Through My Brother's Lens

A JOURNEY OF LIFE LESSONS

Stephanie Maria Moulis

Trilogy Christian Publishers

A Wholly Owned Subsidiary of Trinity Broadcasting Network

2442 Michelle Drive

Tustin, CA 92780

10 9 8 7 6 5 4 3 2 1

Library of Congress Cataloging-in-Publication Data is available.

ISBN 979-8-89041-913-2

ISBN 979-8-89041-914-9 (ebook)

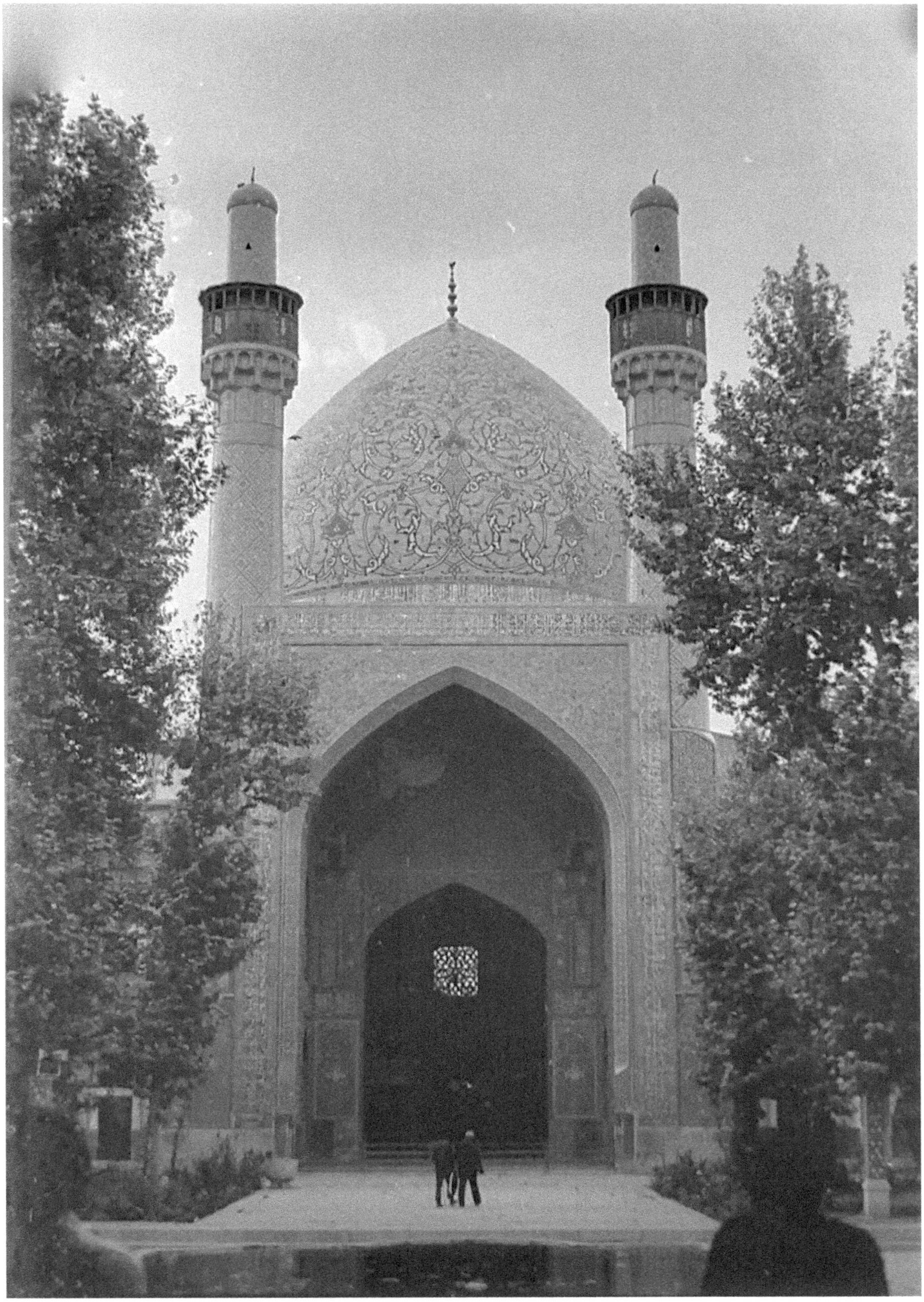

"The show must go on." (PT Barnum)

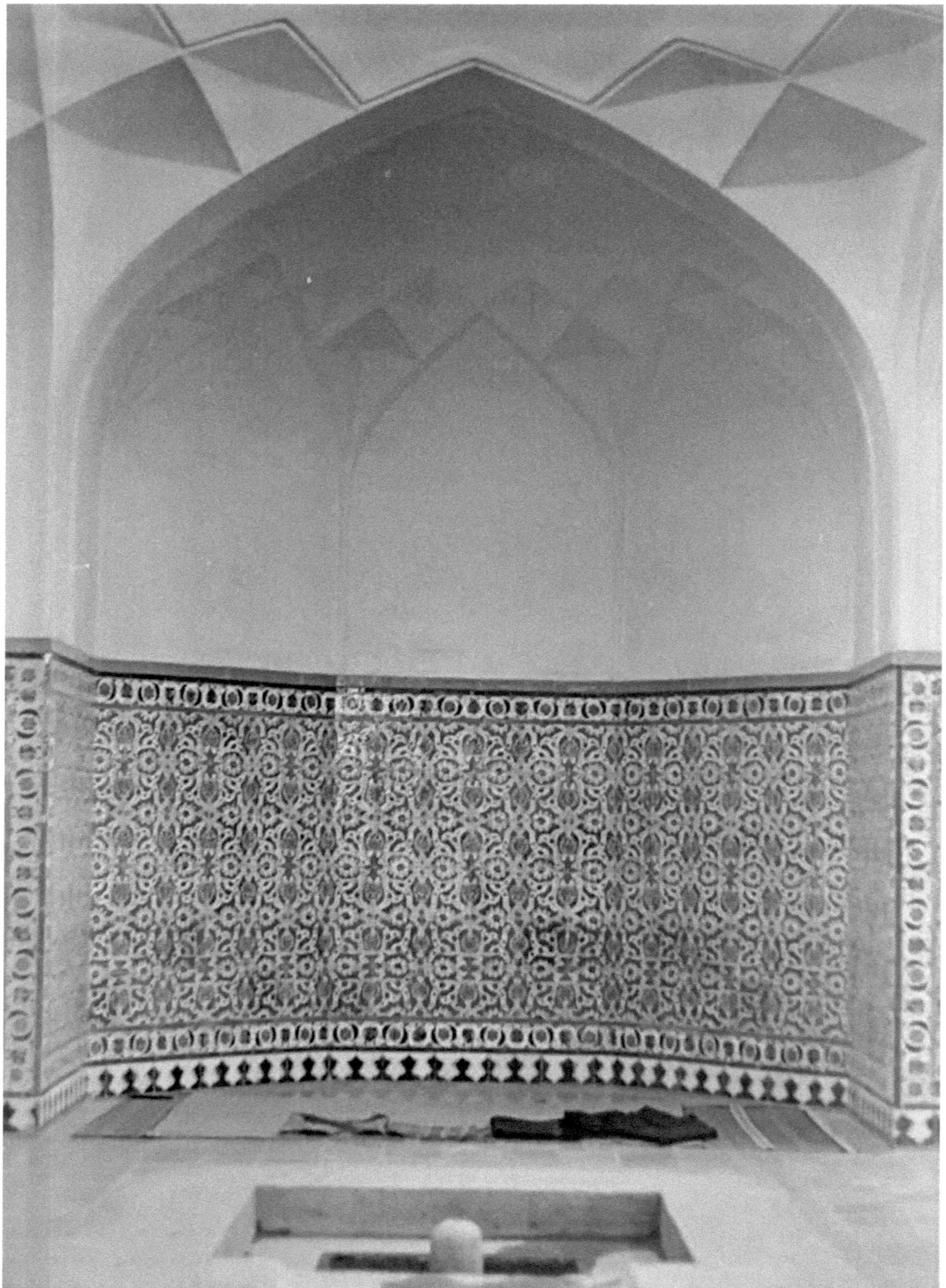

Photos by Dr. Harry Moulis
December 12, 1960 – November 17, 2020

This book is dedicated to my phenomenal brother
His amazing legacy is like no other

This truly has been a labor of love
My inspiration came from above

Thank you sincerely for your support of this endeavor
I hope you'll find my interpretation somewhat clever

Proceeds from this book will be donated to his church
As well as to brain cancer for further research

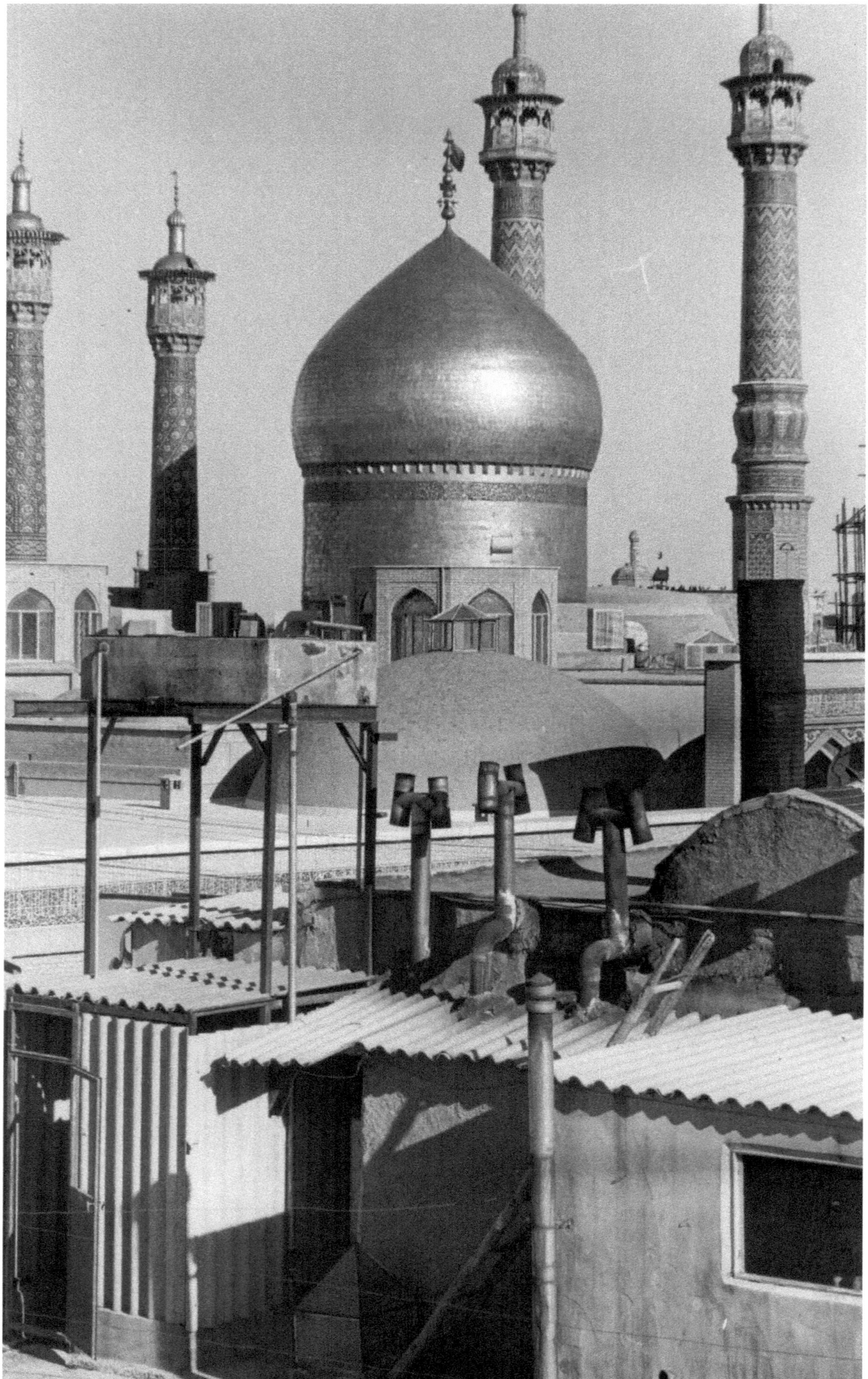

Thank you sincerely...

To God for providing me with guidance and strength

To my late brother, Harry Moulis, whose photos and courage inspired me to write this book

To my sister-in-law, Debra Moulis, for taking care of my brother in unimaginable circumstances

To my mother, Helene Moulis, for her unwavering love and encouragement

To my late father, Peter Moulis, whose presence is always in my heart and in this book

To my sister, Aphrodite Moulis, for never letting me give up

To my brother-in-law, David Sutterfield, for his brotherly support

To my cousin, George Vlachos, who helped me bring this book to life

To my cousin, Patricia Fiore, for her generosity and inspiring advice

To my dear friend, Rita Soto, for being there for me through every life lesson

To the late PT Barnum for his insightful quotes

To Father Yuri Brubach and the congregation of Holy Cross Orthodox Church for their prayers

To the Glioblastoma Research Organization for their continued research

To the doctors and staff my brother worked with at Borland-Groover Clinic

To the faculty and students at the American School of Isfahan (ASI)

To everyone who permitted my brother to photograph them in the 1970s

To my publisher, Trilogy Publishing, for taking a chance on a first time author

To the USA where I am grateful to have the freedom to write this book

To everyone who knew and loved my brother

To you, the reader, for your generosity in purchasing this book

(Please forgive the long list...This is my first book)

Introduction

I've never written a book before, so why now?

In 2020 my brother, Dr. Harry Moulis, passed away from glioblastoma, a form of brain cancer with a low survival rate…He was fifty-nine. It was diagnosed in a late stage, and the doctors did not know what caused it. His wife, Debra Moulis, became his caregiver in the midst of the COVID pandemic. My brother's diagnosis and passing was devastating for our family, and I would like to help others who may be going through a similar trauma.

What significance do the photos have?

In addition to being a highly respected Gastroenterologist, my brother was also an avid photographer. His photos have been featured in Daytona Beach, FL at the Twin Lakes Radiology Imaging Center and at the Museum of Arts & Sciences, as well as in prominent publications such as National Audubon Society and National Geographic.

The photos in this book reflect my brother's early days learning photography at the American School of Isfahan in Iran. Our father, an electrical engineer who worked for Grumman Corporation in Long Island, NY, accepted an assignment in 1975 to temporarily relocate to Iran. Our family lived there along with hundreds of other American families for three years with no phone, radio, or television. We formed wonderful friendships, and it was an amazing cultural experience…until December 1978 when we were evacuated. In February 1979, the Shah of Iran was overthrown, which was followed by the Iranian hostage crisis. Iran in the 1970s was a very different place than Iran of today. My brother's photos represent a peaceful bygone era with unique images that capture moments from a once-in-a-lifetime experience.

Why is it in poetry format?

I have to thank our father, Peter Moulis, for that. He started a tradition within our family of writing clever poems for anniversaries and birthdays. Sadly, my dad passed away eleven months after my brother, so I am carrying on the poetry tradition in his memory.

Why are there references to PT Barnum quotes?

My brother attended New College of Florida in Sarasota for his undergraduate studies. The Ringling Circus Museum is also located in Sarasota, and it gave me the idea to use some uplifting quotes from PT Barnum. I wasn't sure if my brother would have approved of my choice until I received two signs: The first sign appeared when I was going through his college papers and came across a Ringling Bros Barnum & Bailey Circus advertisement, and the second sign occurred in Florida when I noticed a New York license plate that said "Excelsior," which PT Barnum referenced in one of his quotes and which I have included in this book. Excelsior means "ever upward" in Latin.

How can this book help?

Two dollars from every paperback and hard cover book sale will be donated to charity, one dollar per book for each of the following organizations:

- Glioblastoma Research Organization for raising awareness and funds in the hopes of finding a cure: www.gbmresearch.org
- Holy Cross Orthodox Church in Ormond Beach, FL, where my brother was an active member and his wife Debra is still active: www.hcaoc.org

In Summary...

Writing this book does not make me an expert; however, it has been extremely helpful in my healing process, and I am hoping it will encourage others too. I am a work-in-progress sharing my journey of life lessons through my brother's lens.

"No one ever made a difference by being like everyone else." (PT Barnum)

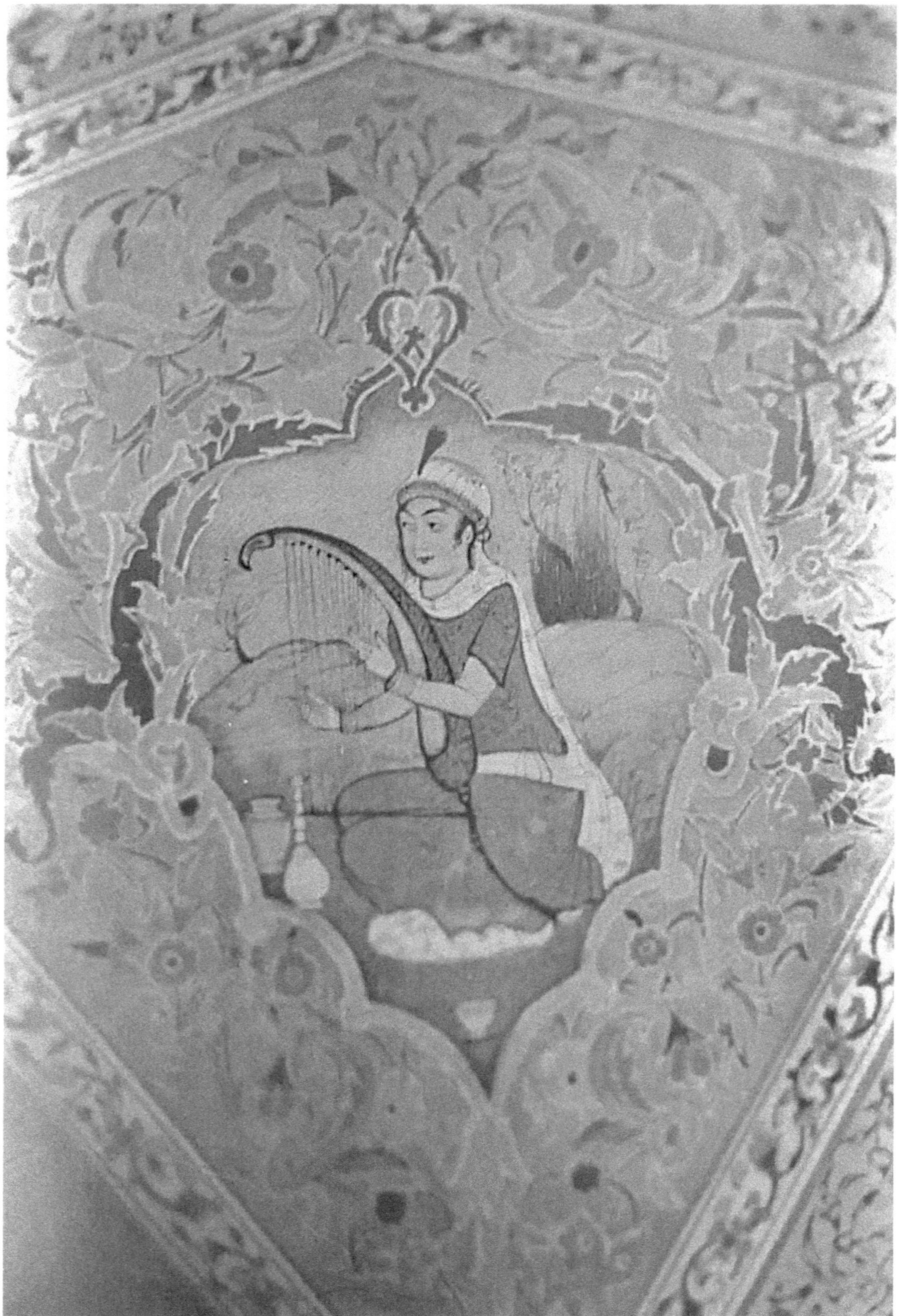

Over forty years ago, in a land far away
Our family embarked on an adventure, which through photos I'll relay

It was the 1970s, and our experiences were unique
The country was Iran, and it was filled with mystique

The photographer was my brother, who was sixteen at the time
What he captured in his photos was truly sublime

Our time on earth is limited, and his was no exception
I created this book in his memory, with all of my affection

This represents my journey of experiencing every feeling
And how it empowered me throughout my process of healing

My hope is that my personal healing transformation
May also fill you with some helpful inspiration

"Take the world and redefine it." (PT Barnum)

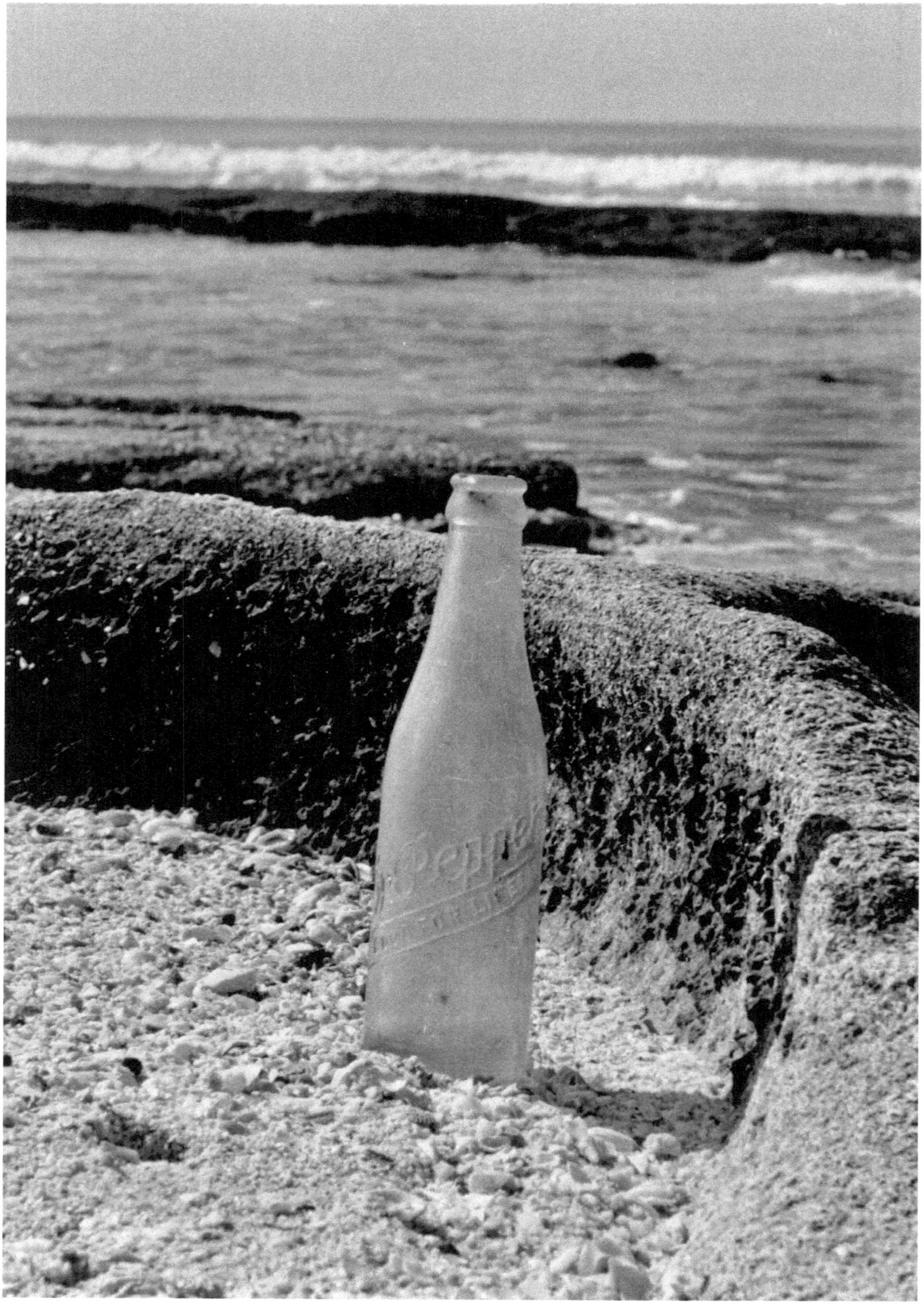

Some may see this bottle as useless and dirty
But underneath the grime, it is remarkably sturdy

Life will give us challenges, of this we can be sure
How we let it affect us sets the stage for what we can endure

Just like in nature, where there is always another season
We must learn to accept the bad times…even when we don't know the reason

Our experiences are meant to make our lives richer
Just like the beauty my brother saw when he took this picture

"When a man is in the right path, he must persevere." (PT Barnum)

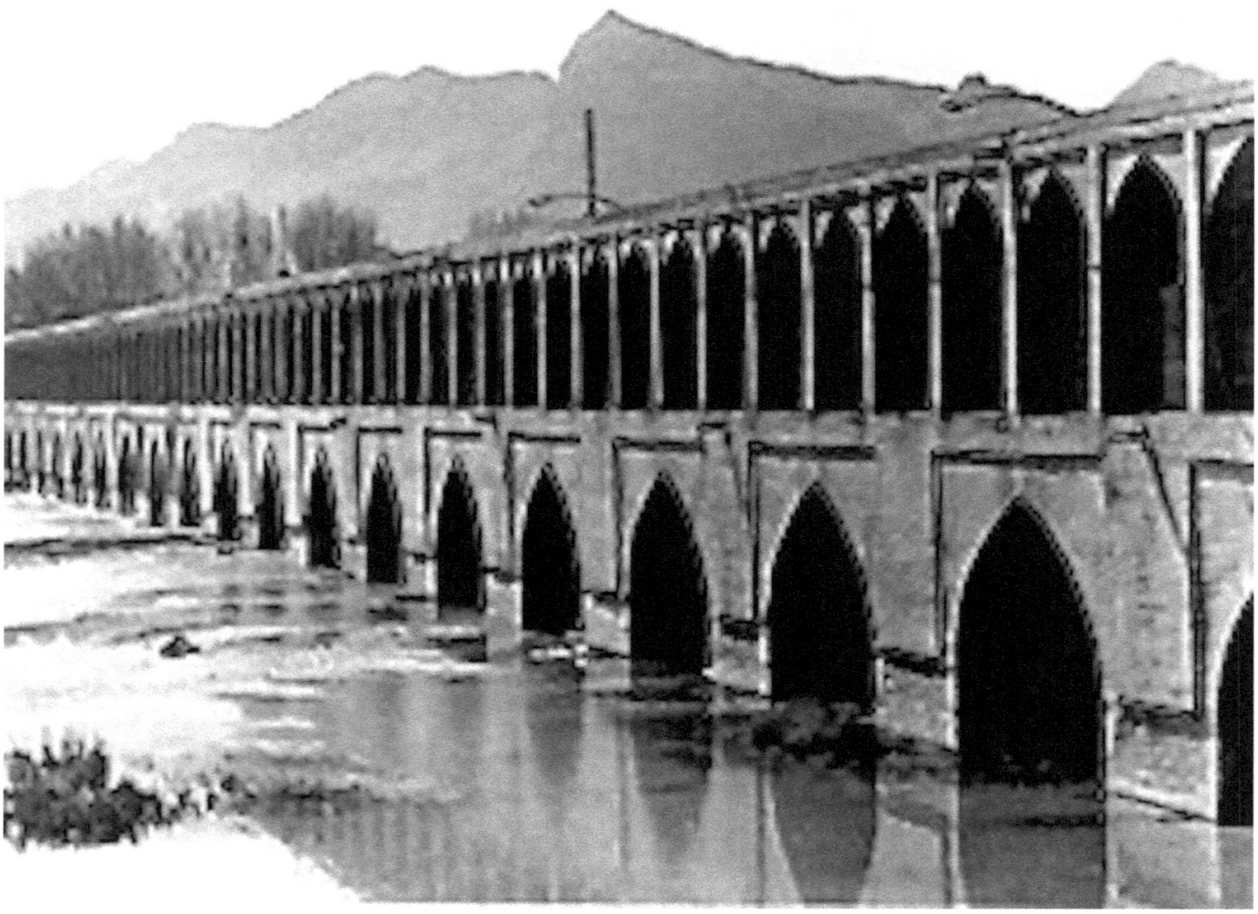

Let's remember our past, but do not regress
Learn from the mistakes we've made and progress

We may encounter the same obstacles time and again
It's so we can master the lesson…we decide when

There is no such thing as failure if we still persevere
As long as we don't let ourselves be controlled by fear

Like crossing a bridge to reach a destination
Our past mistakes propel us to our future salvation

"The best kind of charity is to help those who are willing to help themselves."
(PT Barnum)

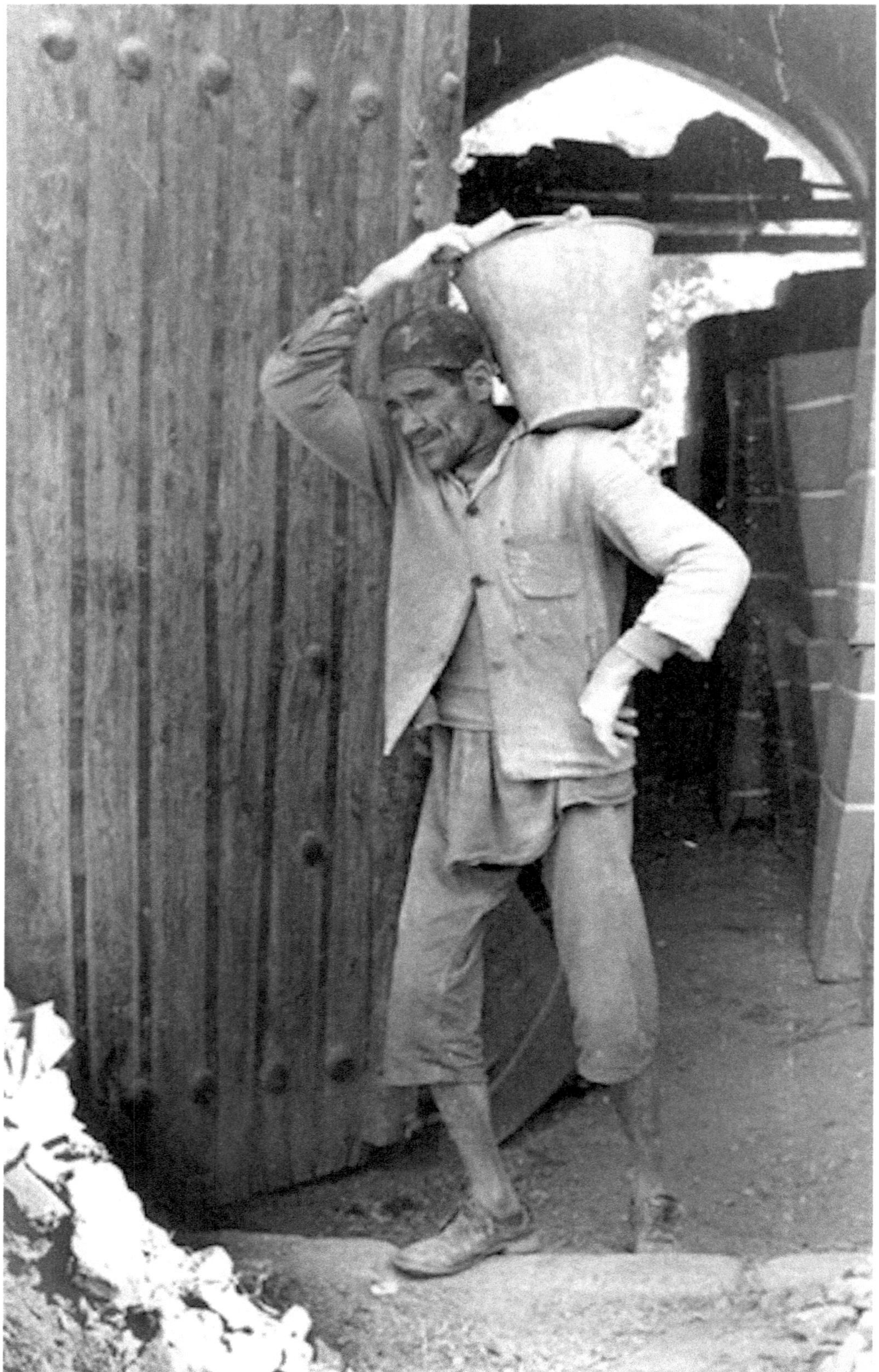

The timing may not be quite what we expect
But one day we'll understand the timing is actually perfect

Every obstacle that is in our way
Gives us more reason to proceed and pray

What we focus on will always grow
So our focus should be on what we can bestow

No matter how small the task may seem
It all helps to drive us towards our dream

"It is the eyes of others and not our own eyes which ruin us." (PT Barnum)

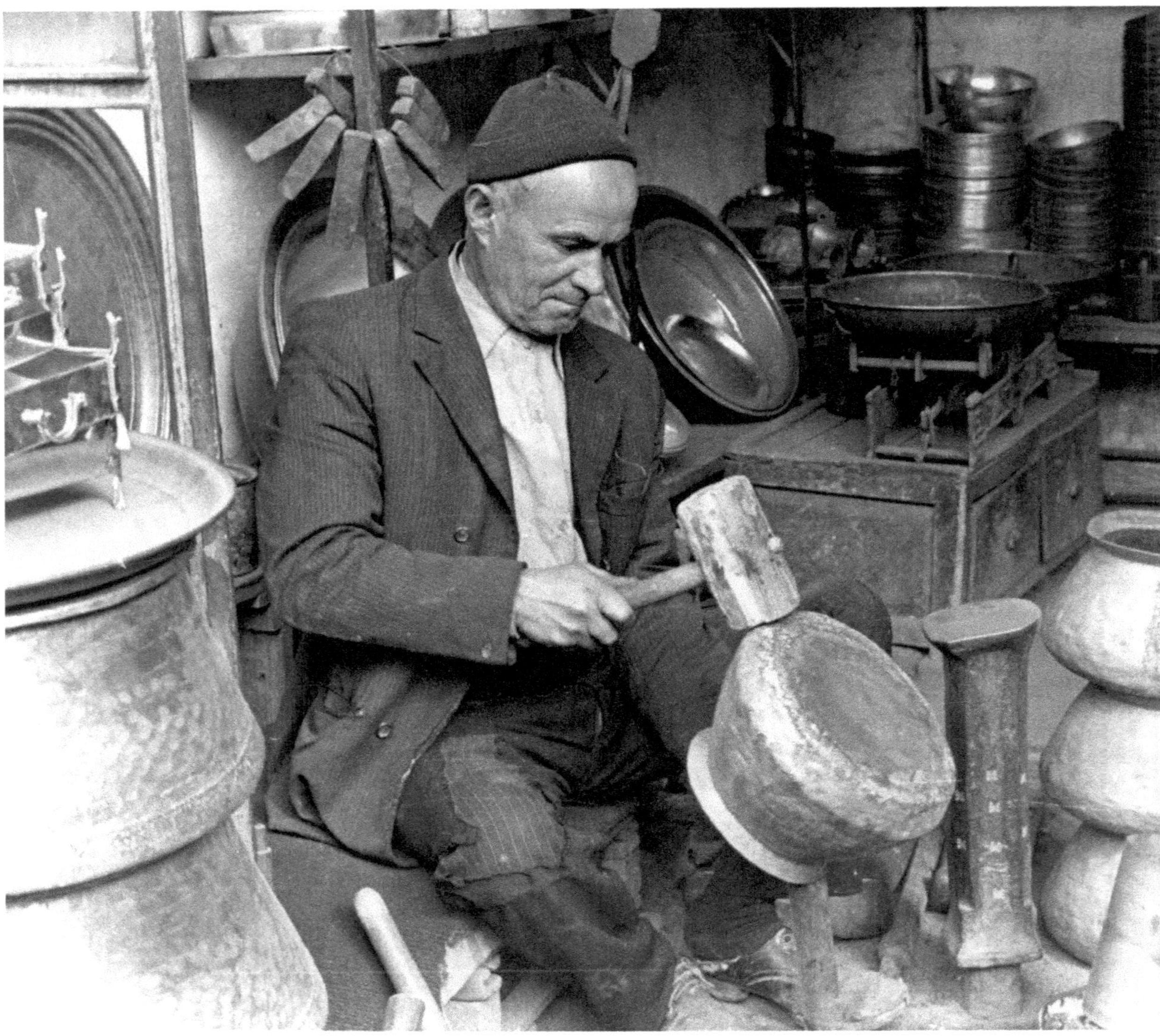

At times we will certainly feel battered and bruised
Which may result in feeling hopeless and confused

Just like metal, which must be shaped and formed
Because of our experiences, we will be transformed

We all have a purpose in life to achieve
So just keep the faith and continue to believe

We must stay true to our authenticity
Allowing life to reward us is serendipity

"Men suffer more from imagining too little than too much." (PT Barnum)

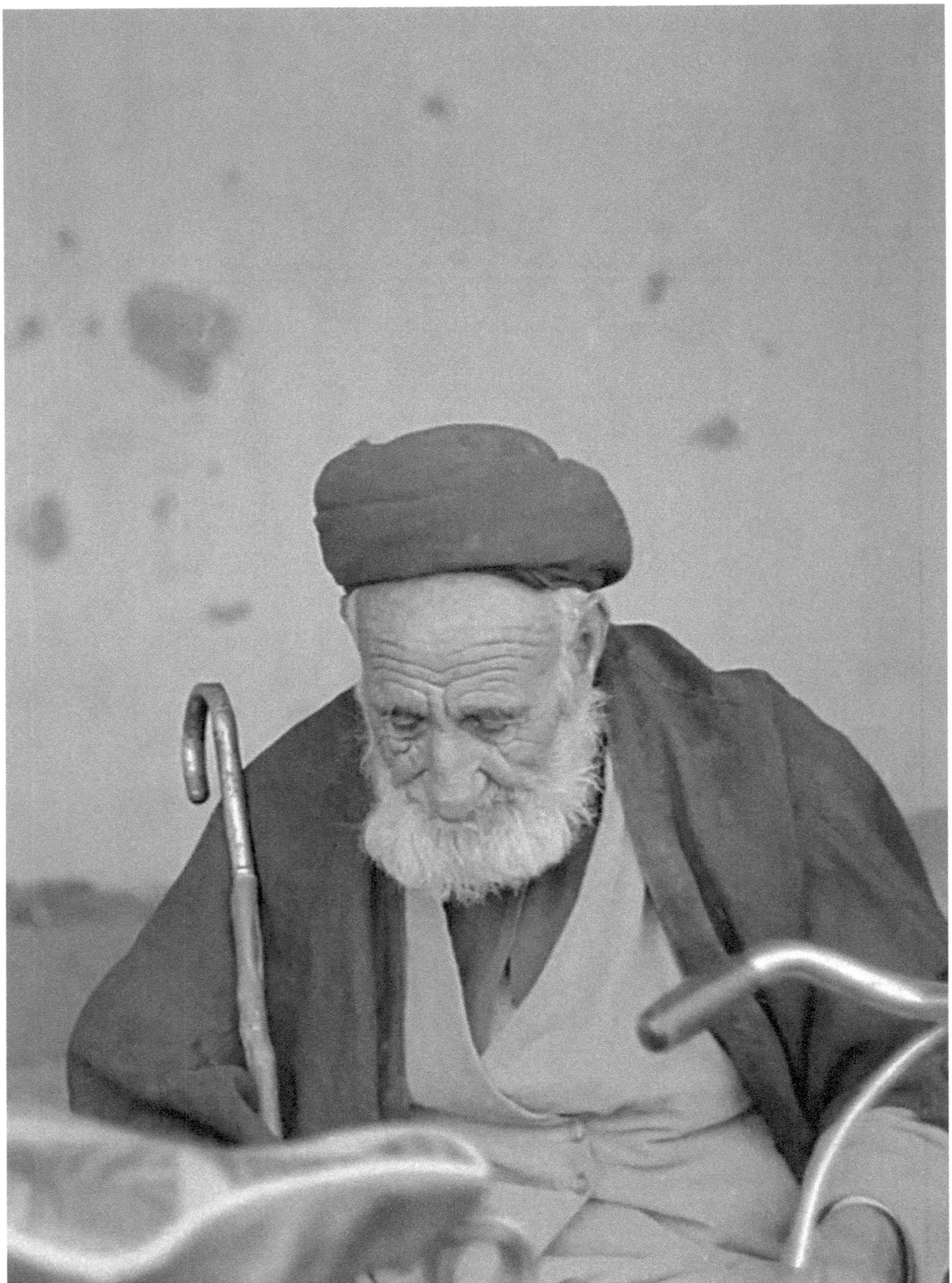

Life goes by so very fast
Before we know it, our present is our past

If there is something in life that we would like to try
We should just go for it without being shy

The more we experience, the more we enhance
The first step is the hardest…so just take a chance

It's best to look back at the risks that we tried
Rather than live with regret…we get to decide

"The foundation of success in life is good health."
(PT Barnum)

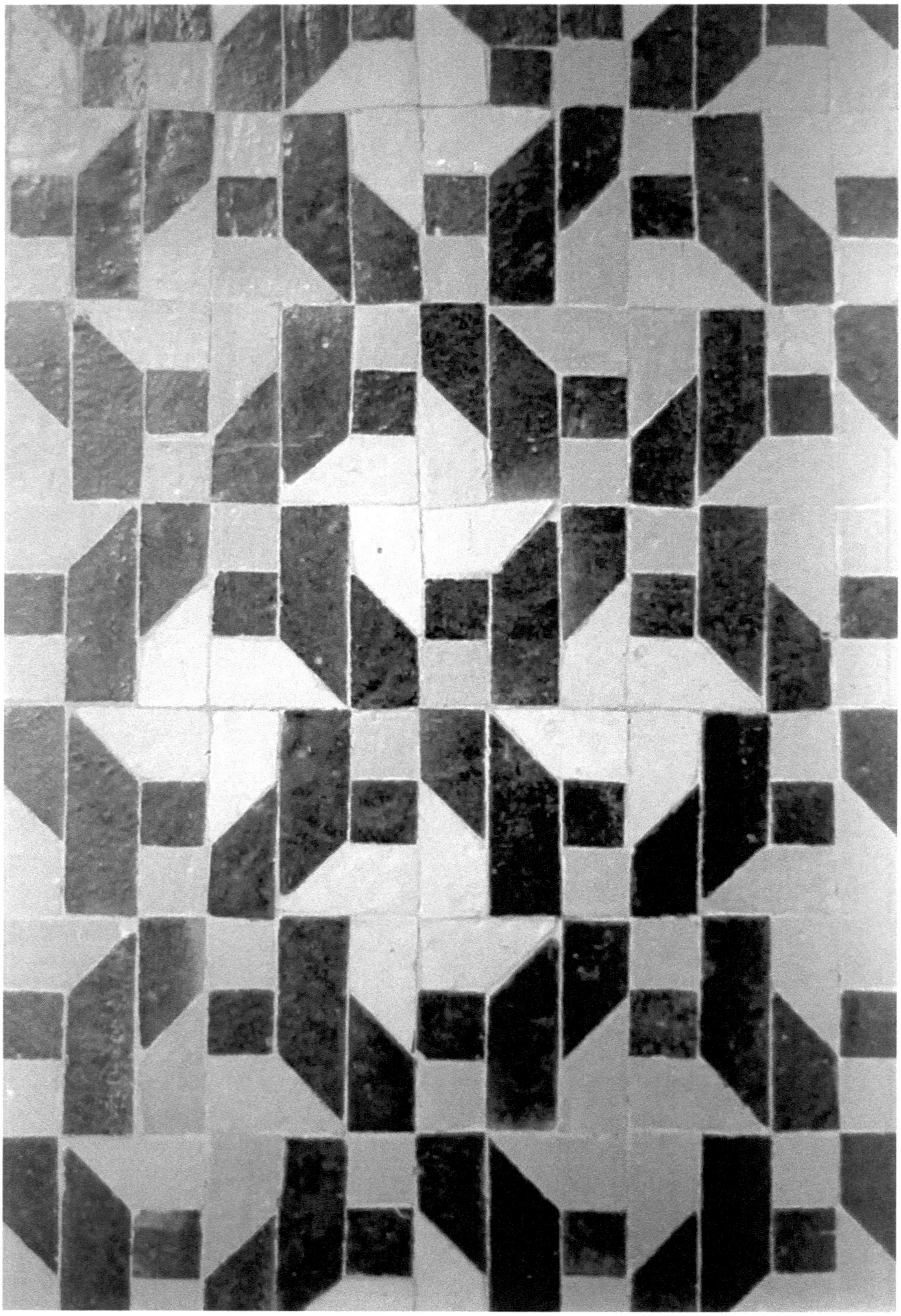

There is no escaping in life that we will all suffer loss
Like the Good Book says, we must bear our cross

These trials test our faith and teach us to persevere
Although during the experience that may not seem clear

Ask for strength and guidance when we meditate and pray
And the light will come even when we don't see a way

The trials we suffer will strengthen our soul
And like pieces of a puzzle, they will make us whole

"Your success depends on what you do yourself, with your own means."
(PT Barnum)

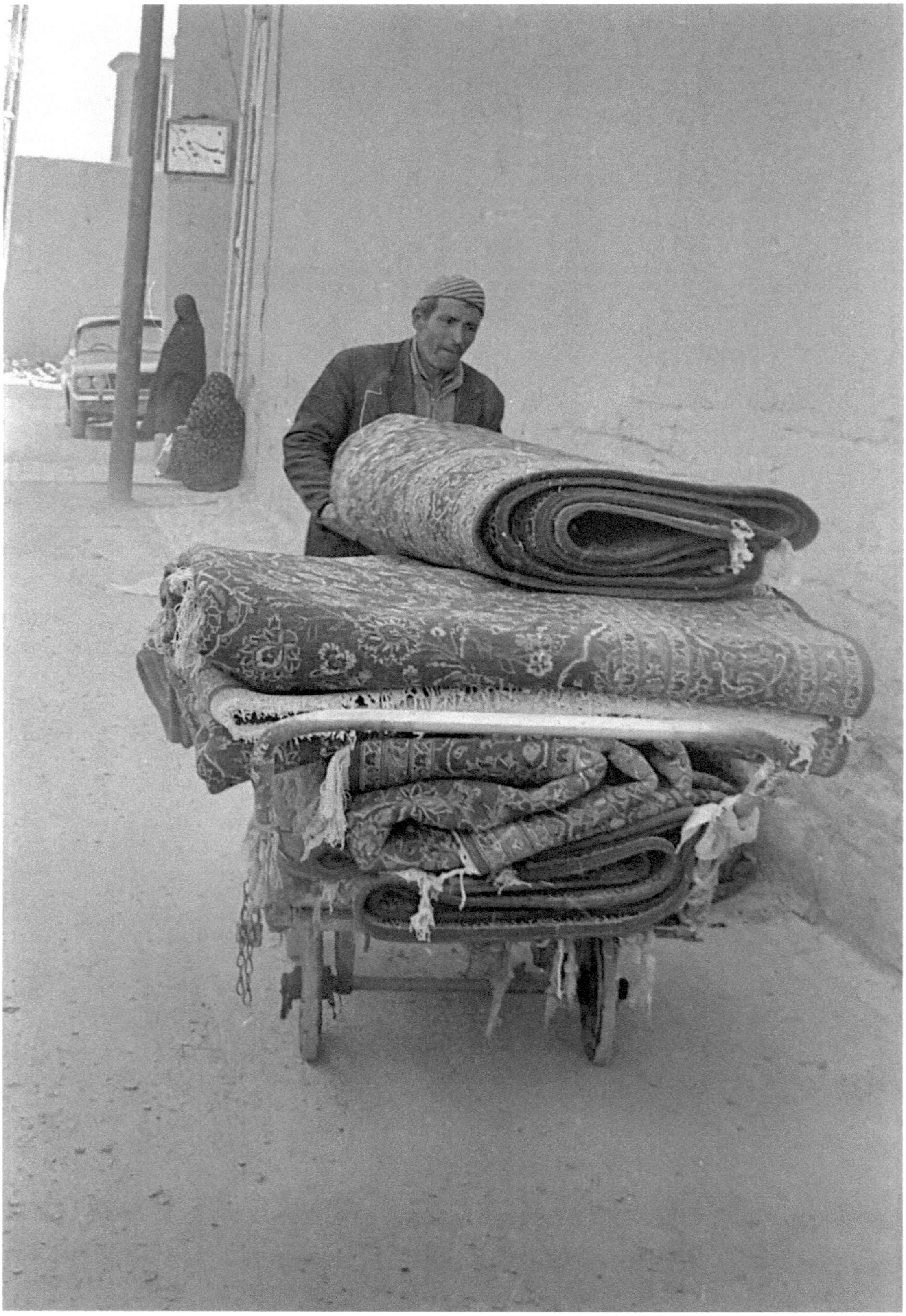

Every trial along the way is there for a purpose
We should appreciate each lesson and not let it deter us

We were put on this earth to become our very best
And to achieve our goals as part of our quest

When there is a dream that we would like to pursue
We must imagine it until it is clearly in view

When we reach deep into our subconscious mind
We realize our life can be completely redesigned

"Comfort is the enemy of progress." (PT Barnum)

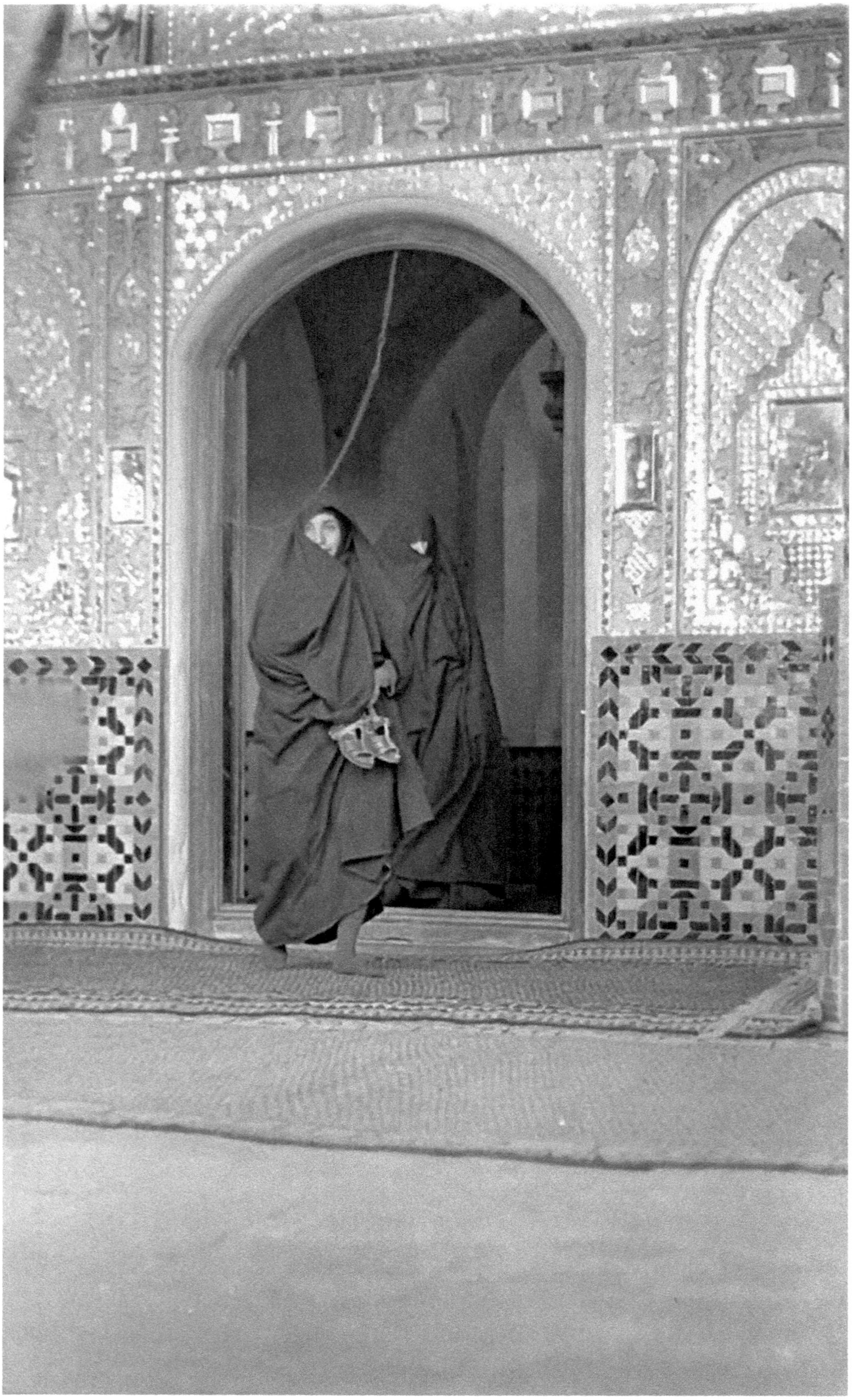

There is only one person with our DNA
We are here for a reason, come what may

They say life begins at the end of our comfort zone
With some courage, it is time to step into the unknown

Any change in life can be a bit scary
But to hide from it would be quite contrary

Those who succeed still experience fear
But they don't let it stop them and they still persevere

"If you hesitate, some bolder hand will stretch out before you and get the prize." (PT Barnum)

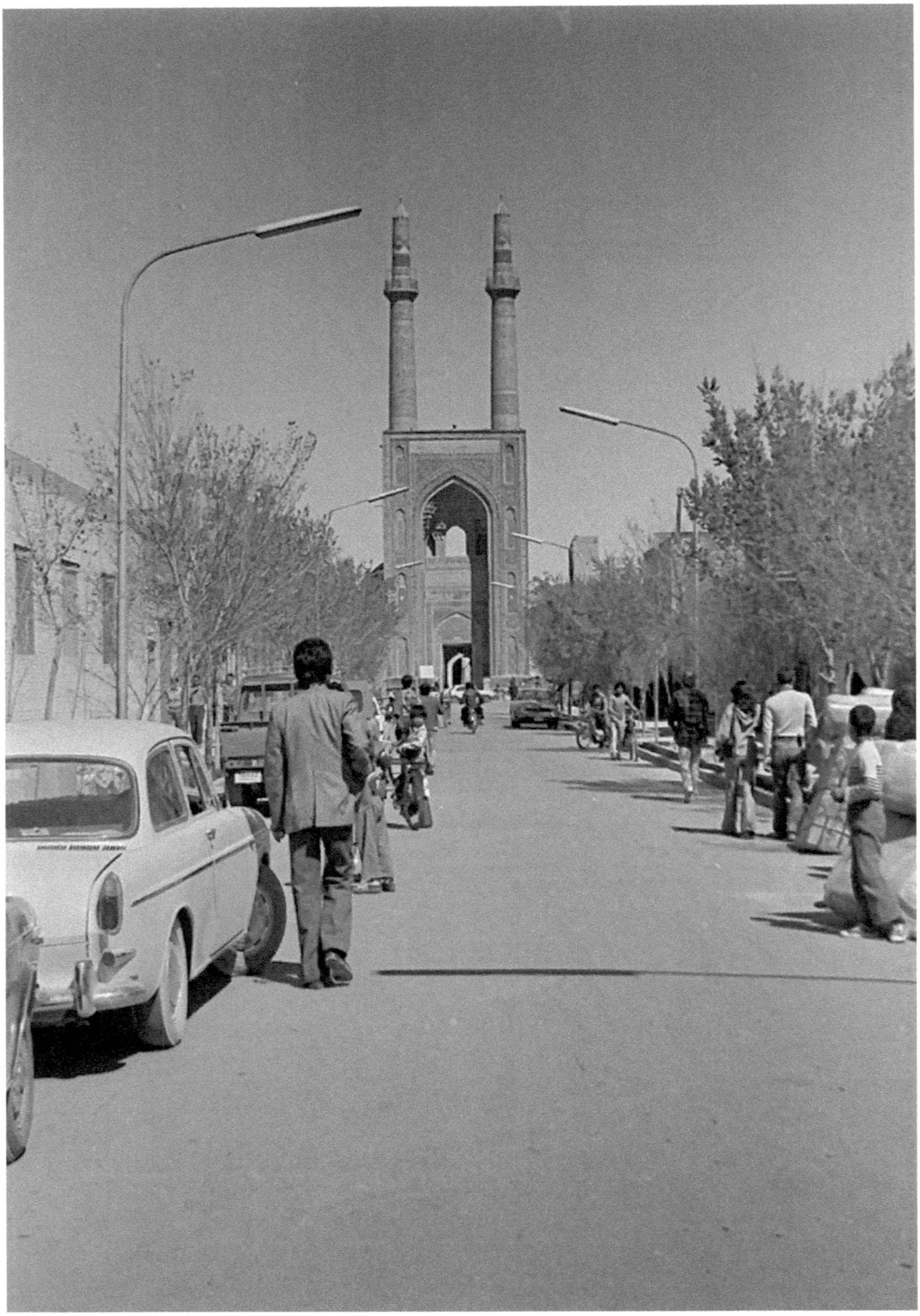

Life is a journey, that much is true
If there is a path not taken, why not pursue?

Our world is full of extraordinary history
It is up to us to explore the unknown mystery

We may not know what lies before us
Yet a proper mindset will help to restore us

We should focus on visualizing our future circumstances
And with active faith, we must take chances

"You must exercise your caution in laying your plans,
but be bold in carrying them out."
(PT Barnum)

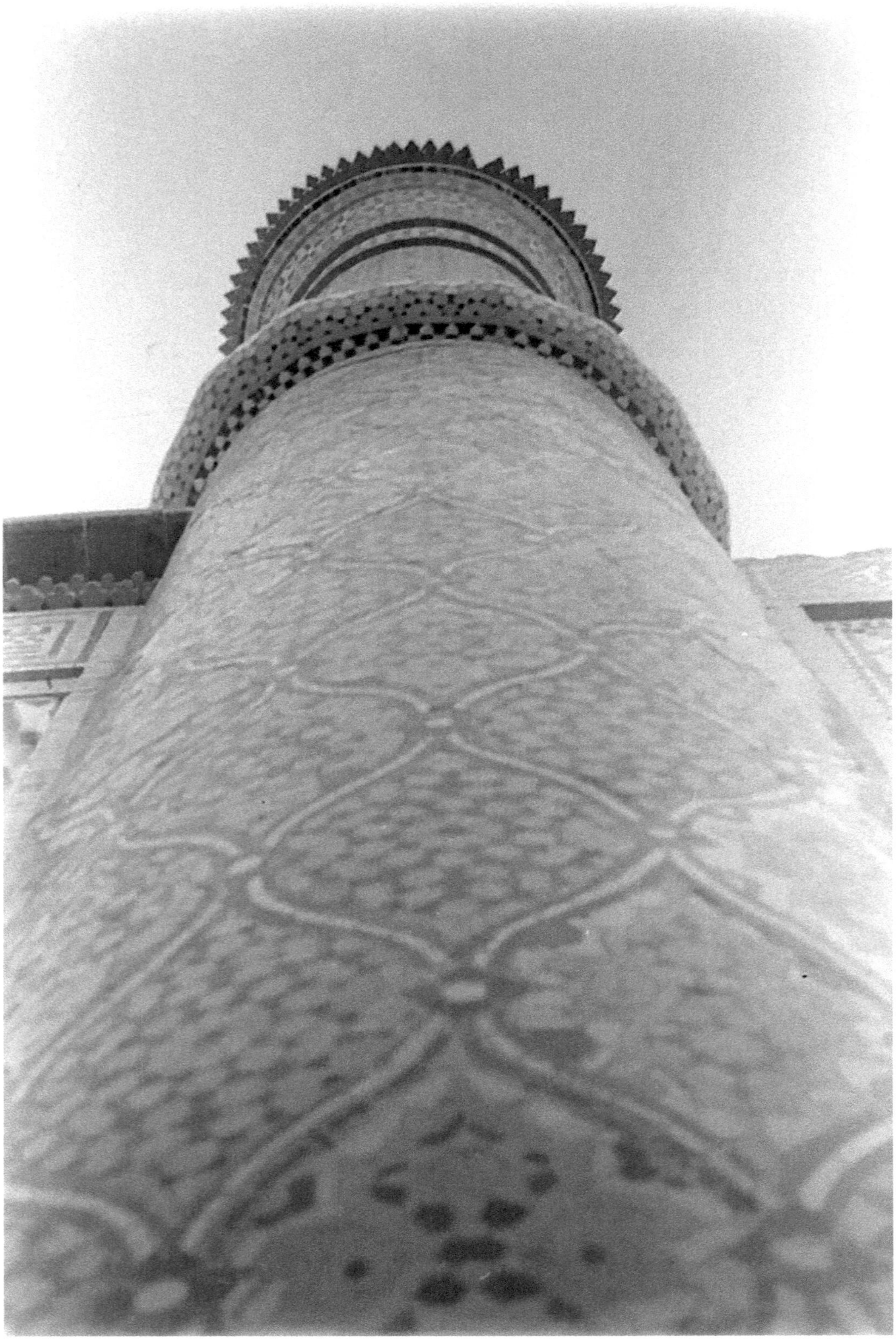

Although our ideals may seem too far beyond
Our minds have the ability to respond

Let's not worry about how it could possibly transpire
Just endeavor and remain true to our desire

Keep our focus on our destination
And envision ourselves there in our imagination

Our minds are capable of more than we know
As long as we challenge ourselves, we will continue to grow

"There is no such thing in the world as luck."
(PT Barnum).

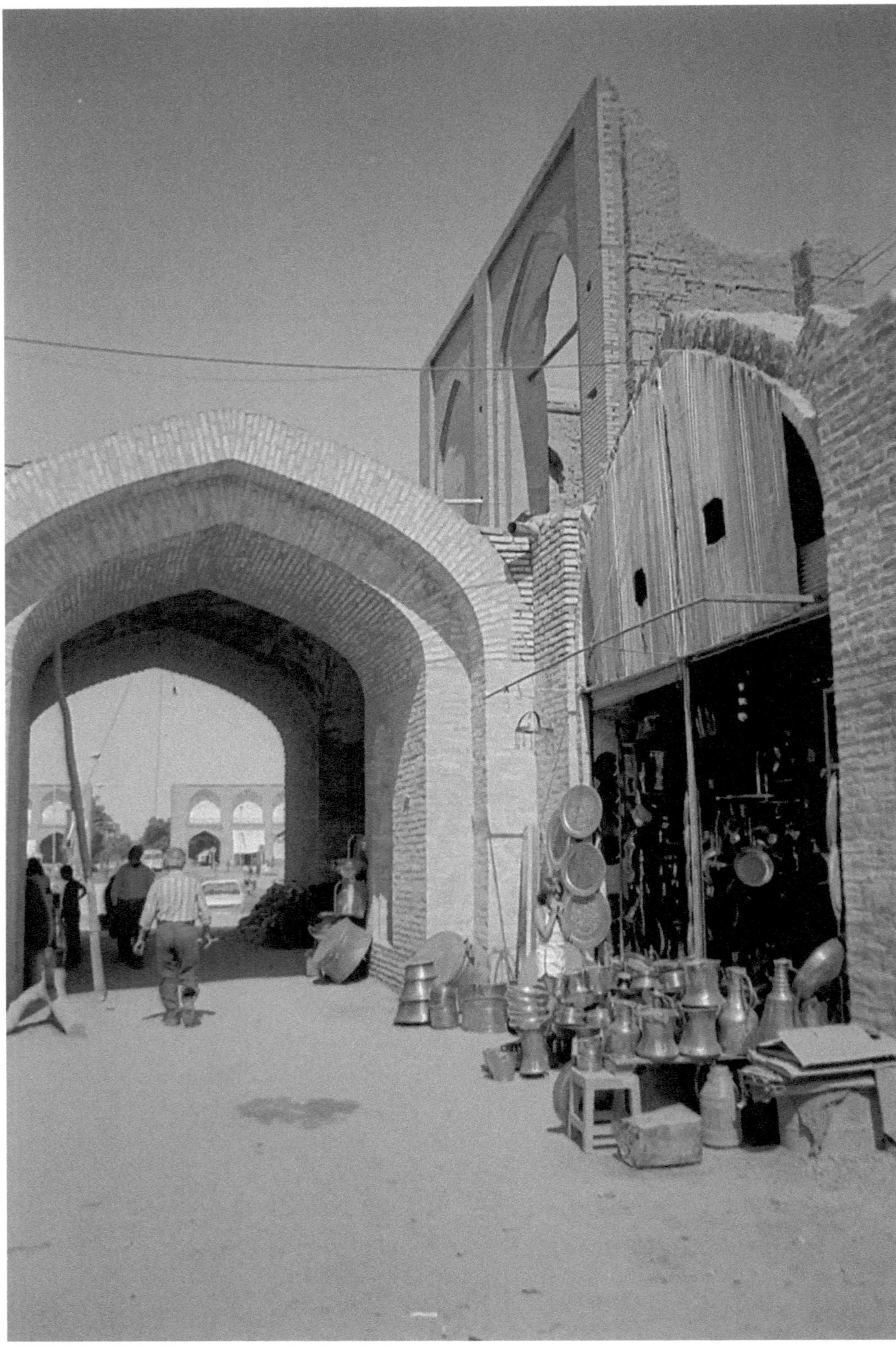

Travel when the opportunity arises
And we'll experience a world of surprises

Exposure to different cultures will definitely enrich us
Especially when we are inquisitive, open, and ambitious

There is a reason the world is so dynamic and diverse
Let's absorb each culture and let ourselves immerse

Life is what we make of it, and adventure awaits
And with every adventure, we enhance our fates

"Those who really desire to attain an independence, have only to set their minds upon it, and adopt the proper means…and the thing is easily done." (PT Barnum)

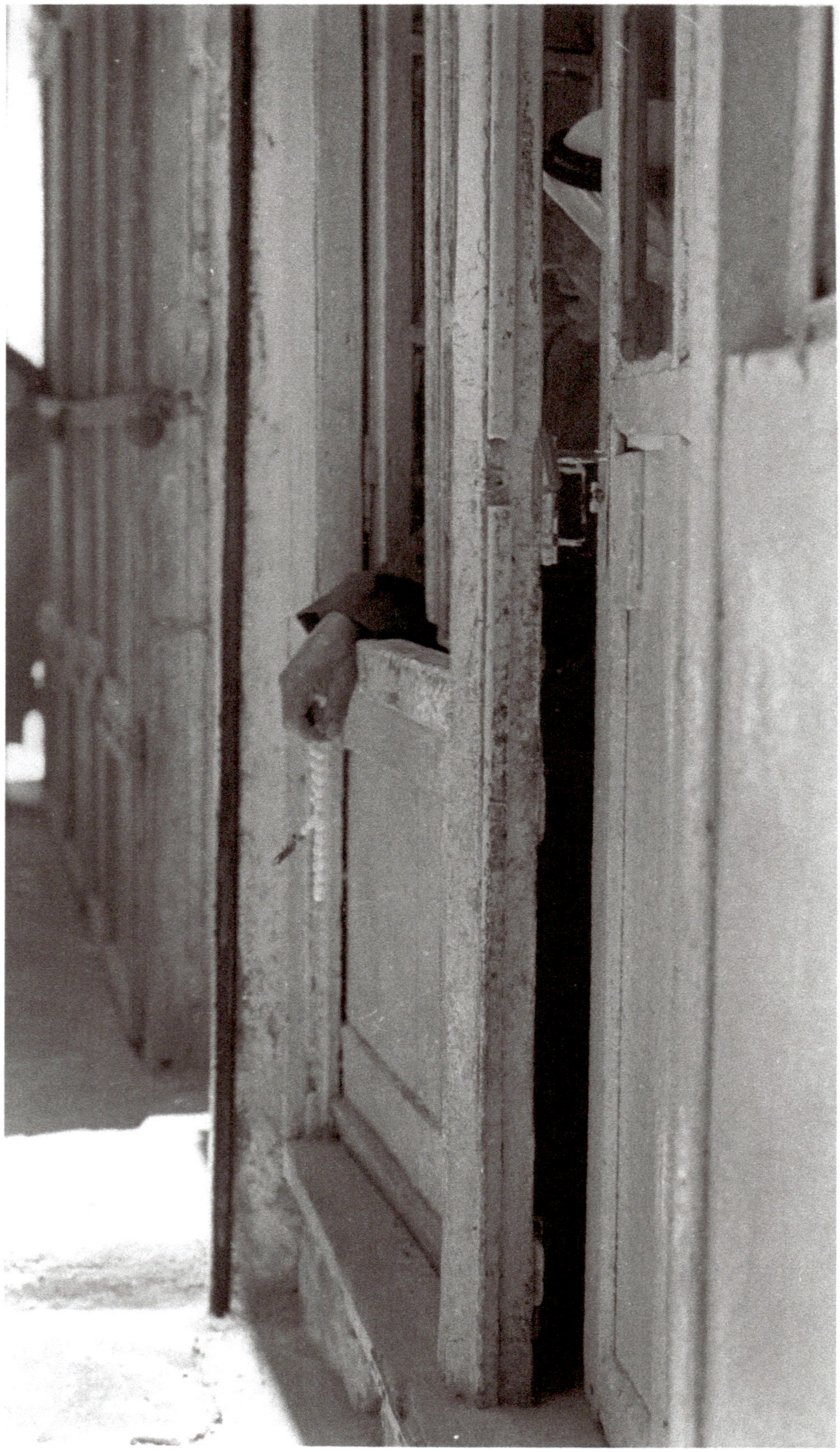

Open and closed doors are always a sign
There are no mistakes from the divine

Behind every door there awaits a surprise
Sometimes our blessing may be in disguise

It may be a change from what we expect
Let's keep our minds open before we reject

The goal that we dreamt will still come to play
But it may come about in an unexpected way

"If I shoot at the sun, I may hit a star." (PT Barnum)

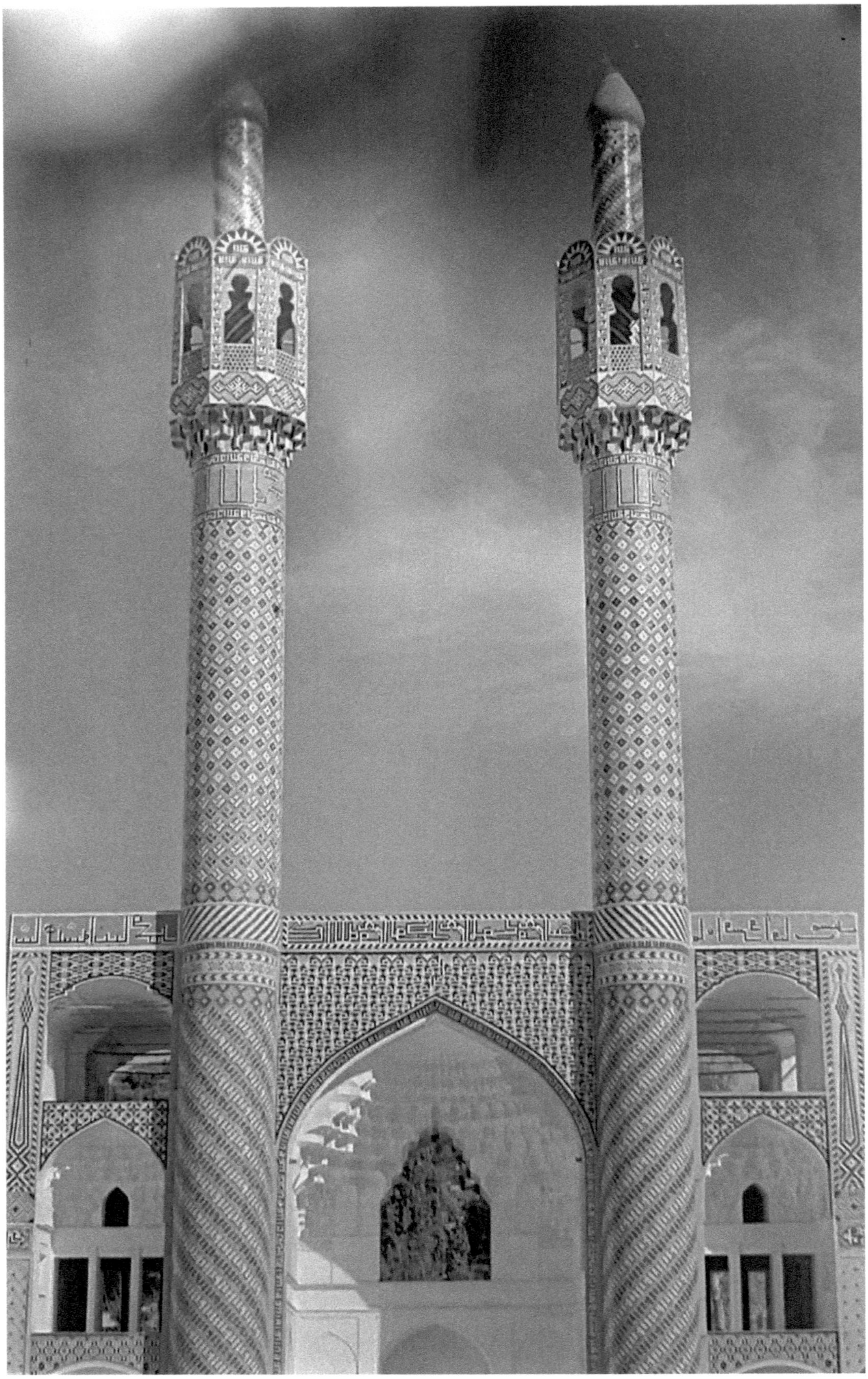

The universe rewards our dedication
To the visions we have in our imagination

Our thoughts are evident when we look around
When we are observant, miracles abound

Our unique destiny is always in motion
Our results are based upon our devotion

When we empower our minds, we can design our fate
The creative force within us is truly innate

"The noblest art is that of making others happy."
(PT Barnum)

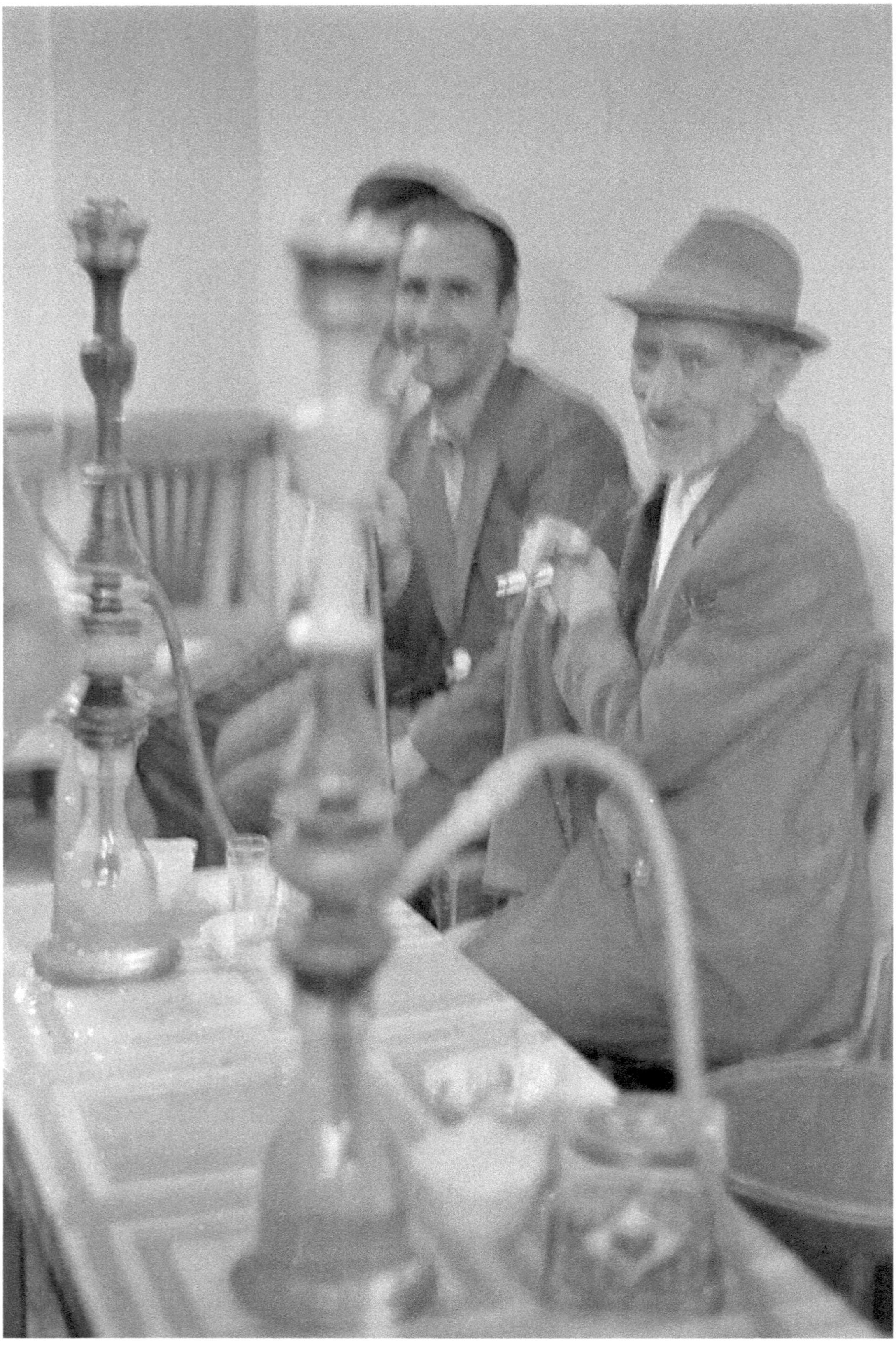

Happiness is a state of mind
We can choose our emotions, so why not be kind?

What may seem unfair will work itself out
If we focus on harmony without any doubt

The trick is to visualize and expect to achieve
Because we can receive as long as we believe

Believe in miracles, they are in every direction
Just be observant through our detection

"Many people are gullible, and we can expect this to continue." (PT Barnum)

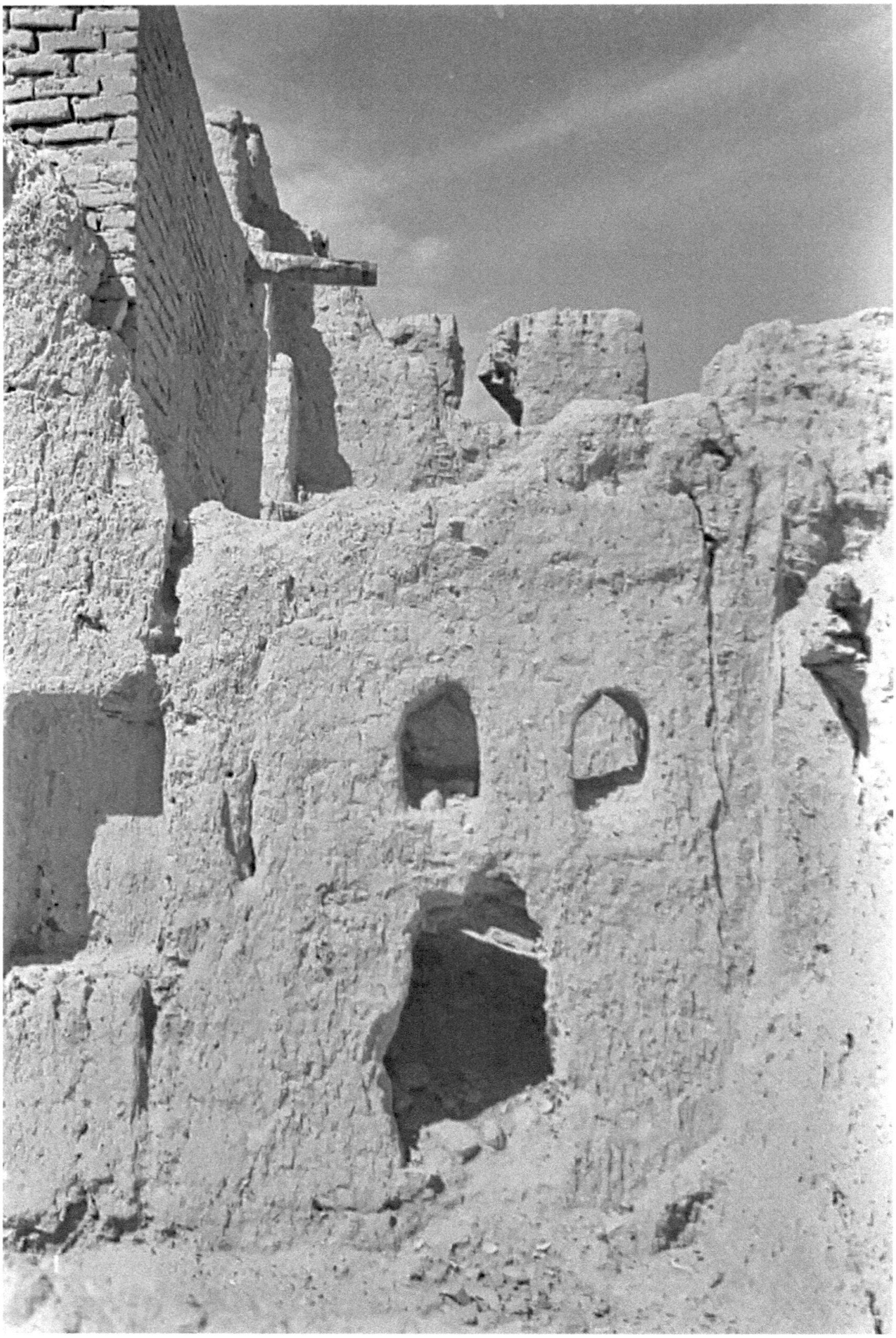

They say the eyes are the windows to the soul
Let others earn our trust and don't give them control

Pay attention to people's actions more than what they say
They can promise the world, but what do they convey?

Just like shattered panes of glass
Broken promises show a lack of class

Let's associate with those who are true to their word
And make sure our opinions are also being heard

"There is a sucker born every minute." (PT Barnum)

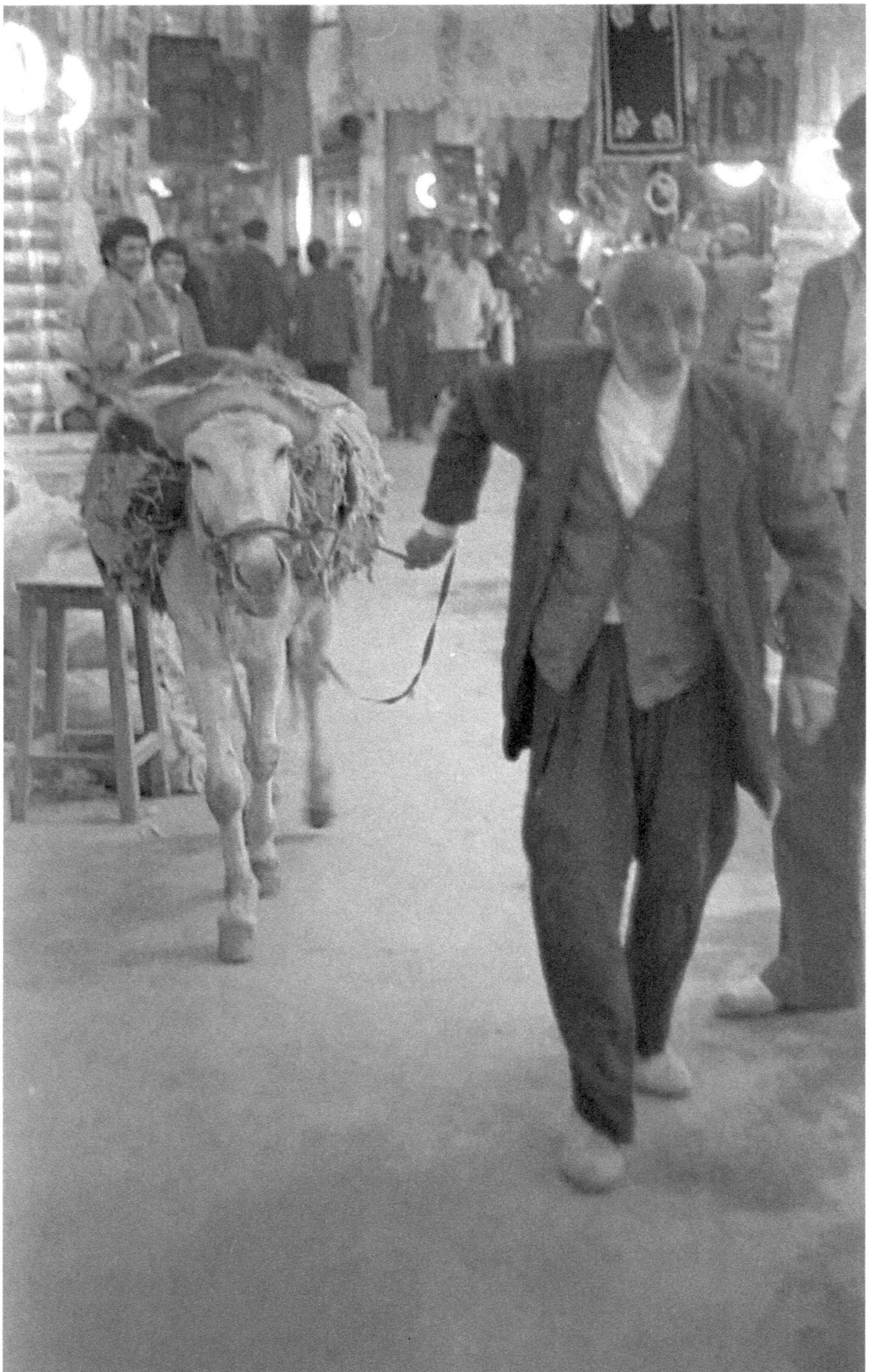

Some act like the animal in this photograph
Mistreating others like common riffraff

It's not a reflection on us, but on them
Pray for their soul rather than condemn

People will treat us the way we allow
Let's reflect our self-worth, starting right now

Hold our heads high and follow our gut
Even if they act like a you-know-what

"To forgive heals the wound, to forget heals the scar." (PT Barnum)

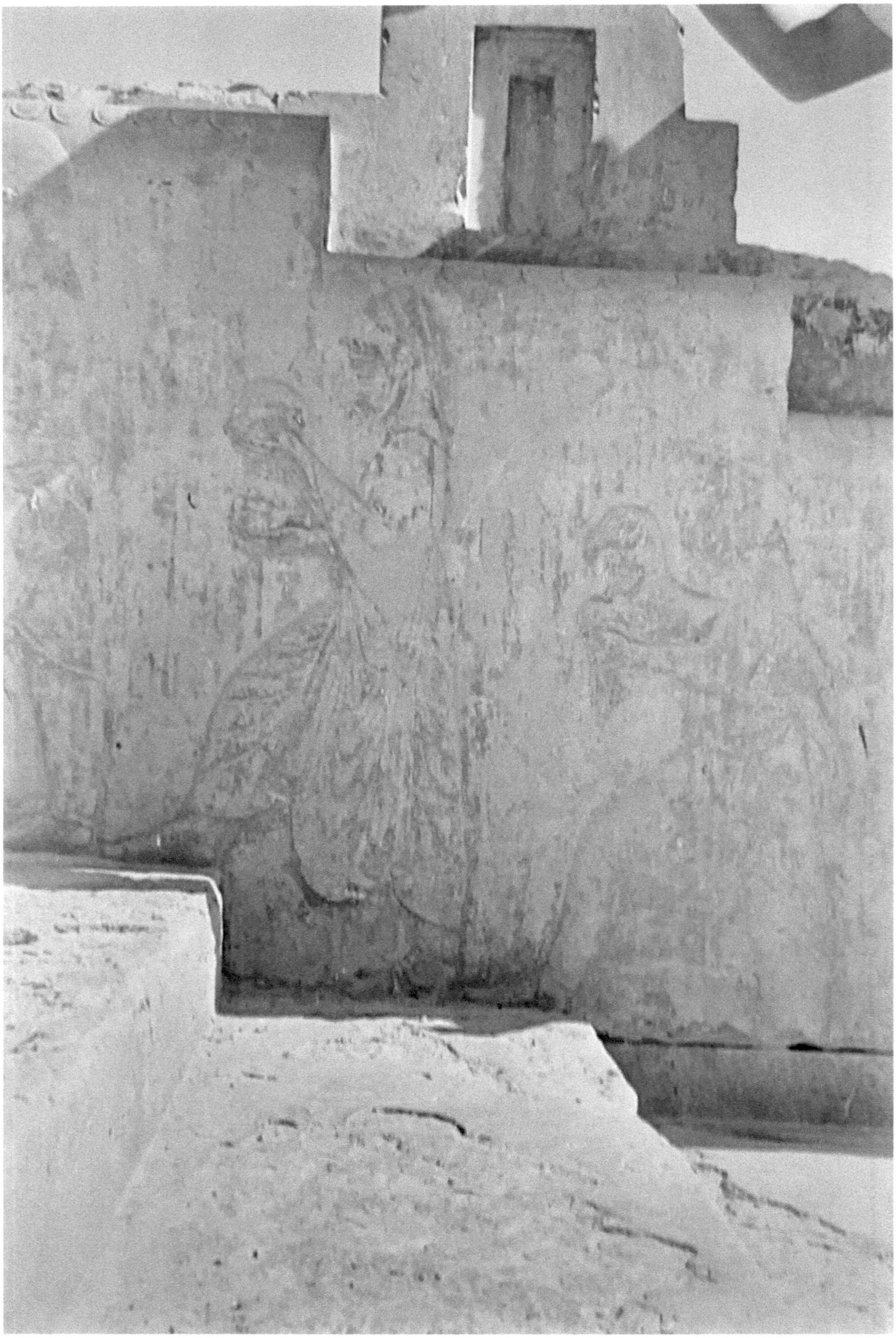

Although the way we are treated may be cruel
We still must live by the Golden Rule

It takes more than attitude to live without regret
We must also learn to forgive and forget

Release anger and resentment…just put it aside
Focus on healing instead of feeding our pride

Holding a grudge really harms only you
Just let the law of karma ensue

"We generally tend to be followers who let others do our thinking for us." (PT Barnum)

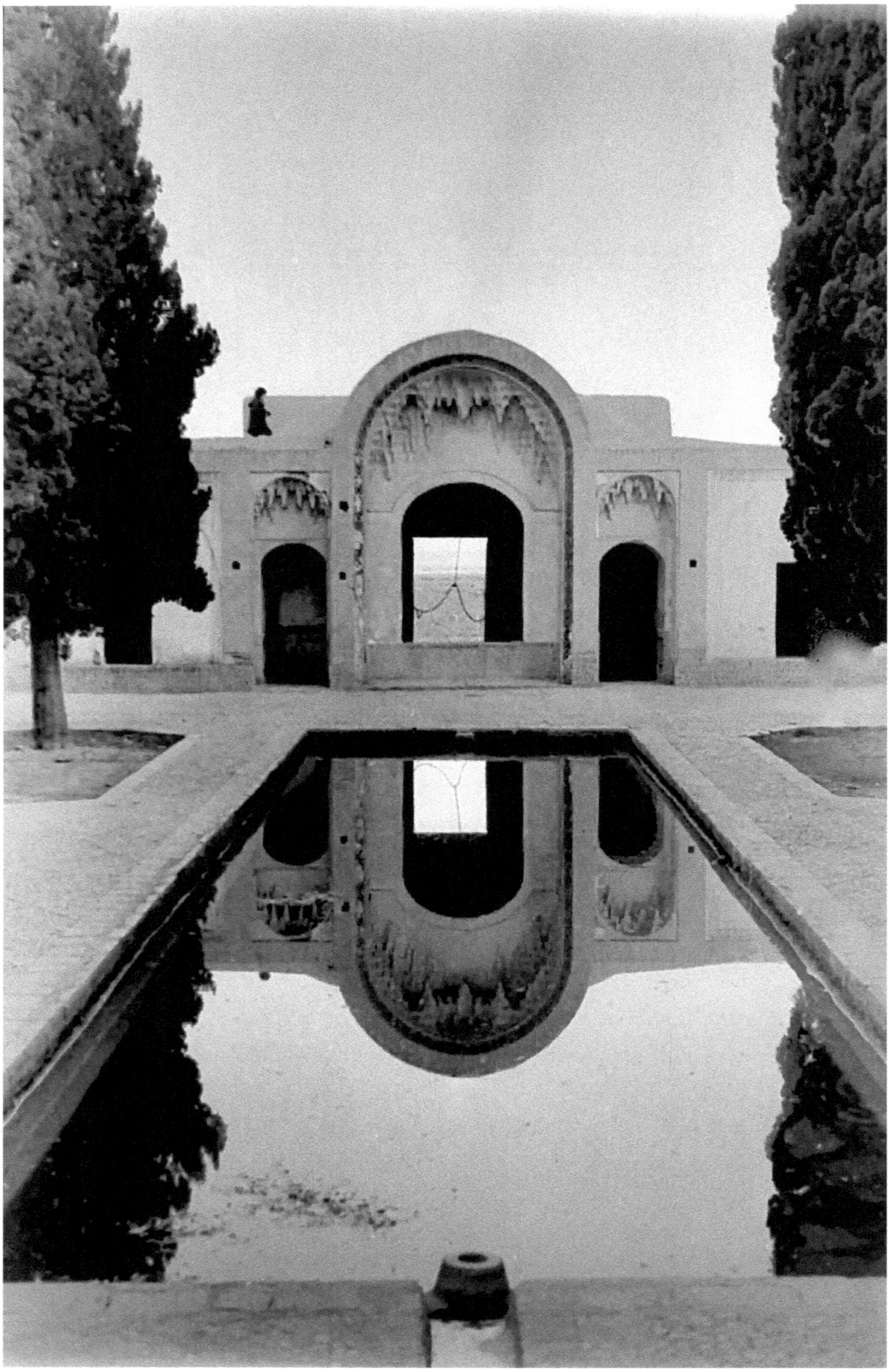

When you look at your reflection, what do you see?
Would you want your thoughts and actions on a marquee?

The only person with you all your life is you
Establish your code of ethics and be sure to stay true

Stand up for what's right and do it with respect
Even when it's not what others might expect

Don't blindly follow what others say and do
Your journey might not be what they went through

"A lovely nook of forest scenery, or a grand rock, like a beautiful woman, depends for much of its attractiveness upon the attendance sense of freedom... upon a sense of purity and of romance." (PT Barnum)

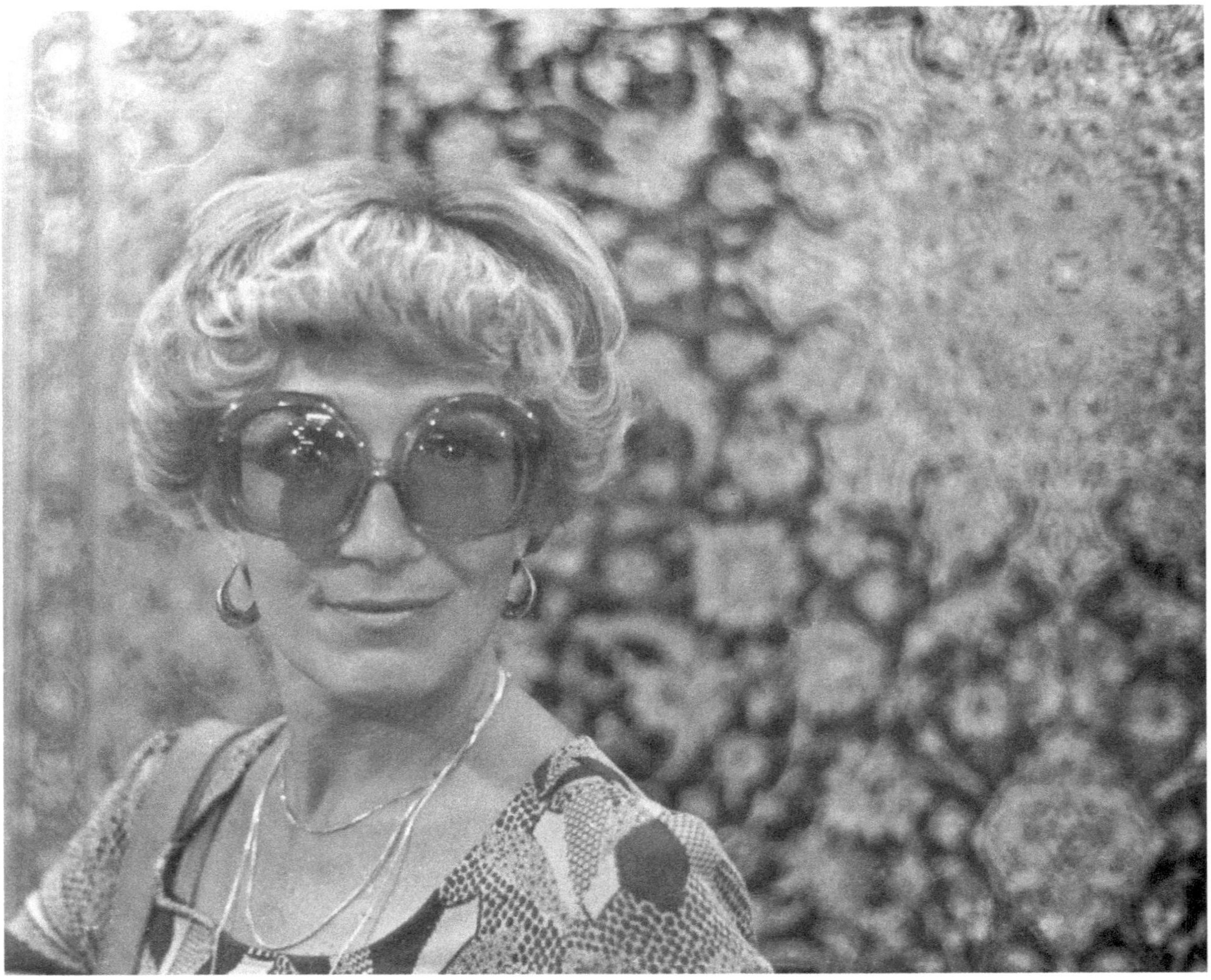

Self-improvement via body, mind, and soul
Establishes confidence and puts us in control

Mastering life with wisdom and grace
Allows us to confidently own our space

We have one lifetime to be our very best
Let's discover our purpose and learn to manifest

Be the best version of you…don't try to be a clone
No one else has your life experiences, so your opinions are your own

"Money is good for nothing, unless you know the value of it by experience." (PT Barnum)

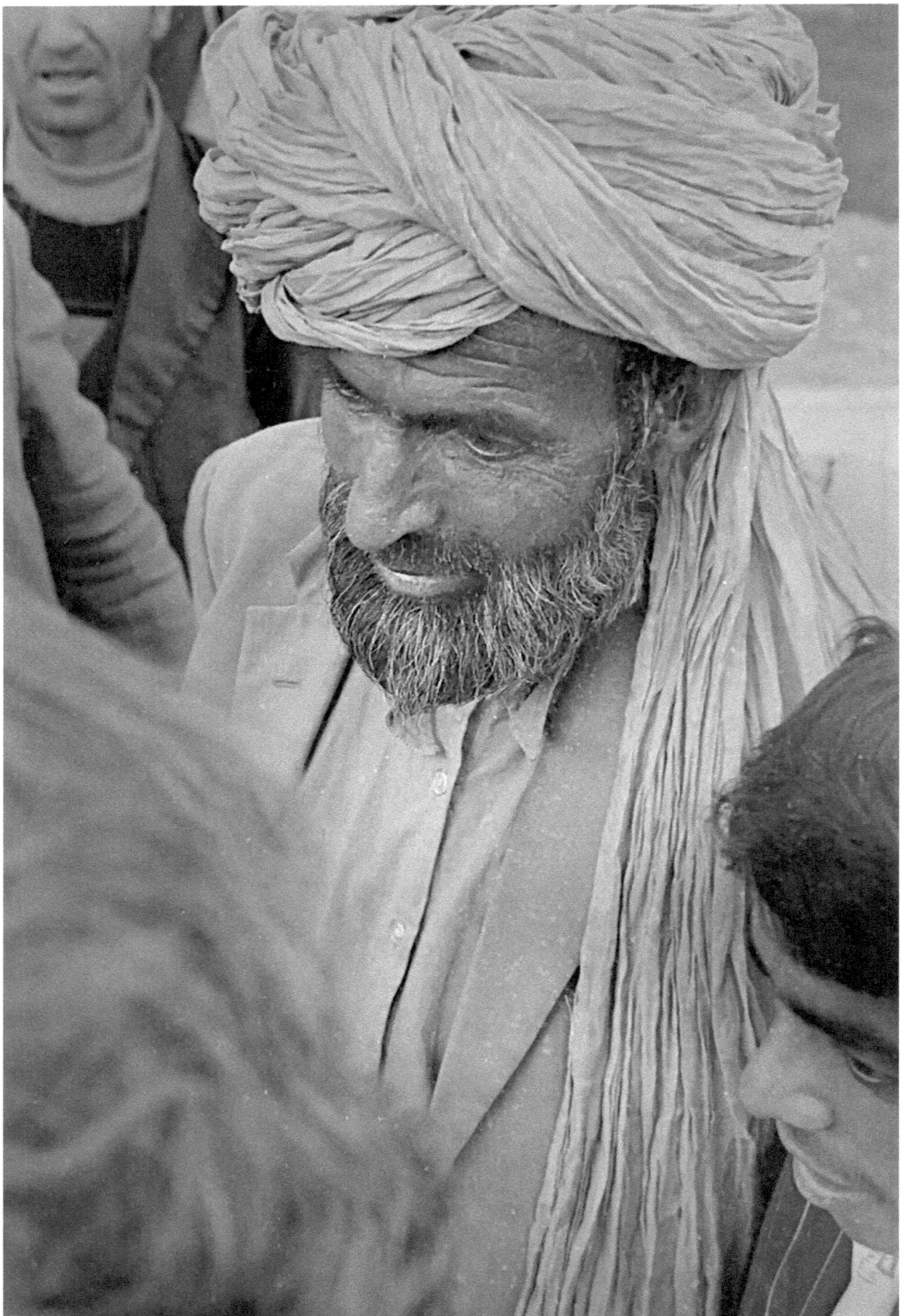

We must stay true to ourselves and not conform
Especially when our objectives are not the norm

We have one life to live, and there is no going back
Be thankful for blessings and don't focus on lack

There is always something to be grateful for
True gratitude results in abundantly more

Enjoy the journey of all of life's wonders
And learn the lessons revealed by our blunders

"I've found the first mistake smart people make is to assume they can't be outsmarted."
(PT Barnum)

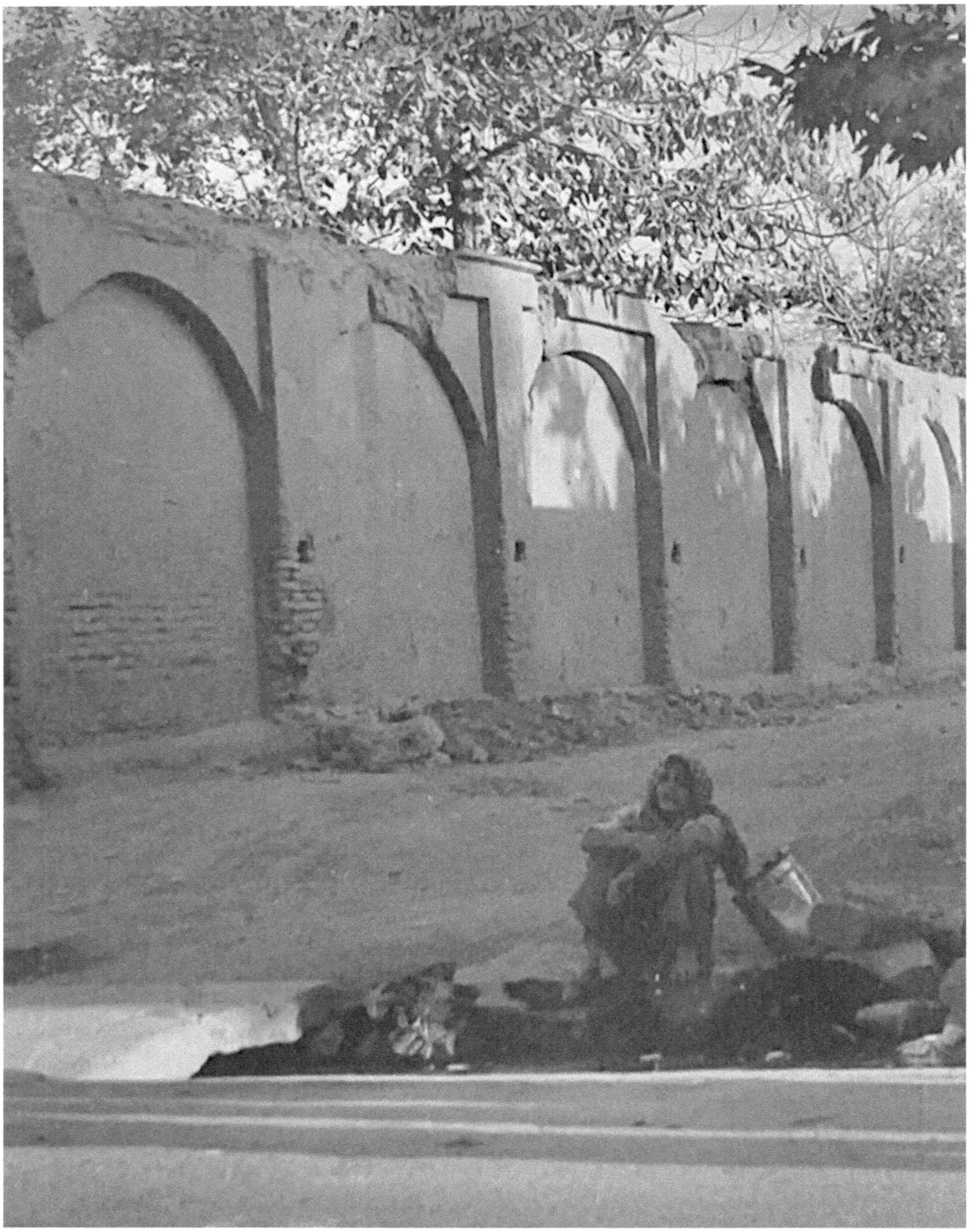

There will be times when we will encounter a wall
And we may be tempted with feelings of withdrawal

Those feelings may manifest into unworthiness and despair
But keeping our goals in mind will eventually get us there

It all starts with a massive change in attitude
Which can best occur when we express true gratitude

Instead of simply reacting and distressing
Embrace every experience as a miraculous blessing

"Without promotion, something terrible happens...
nothing!" (PT Barnum)

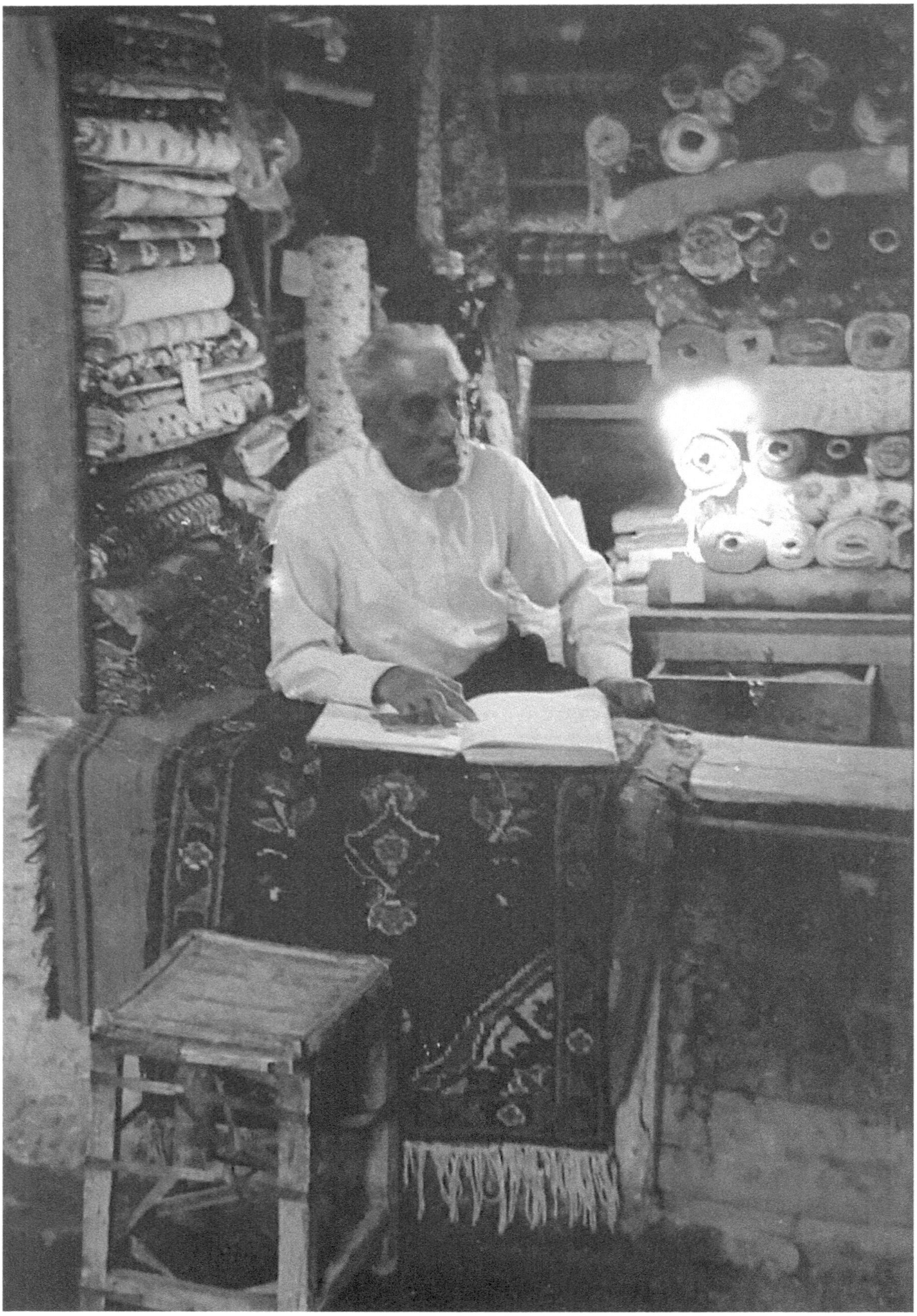

Do not be deterred by any external circumstance
Each one has a purpose, it is not there by chance

We possess more strength than we possibly know
And without the tough times we would never grow

Our limitations are actually self-imposed
Which results in keeping our minds closed

Utilizing sincerity and determination
Truly increases our self-motivation

"We cannot all see alike, but we can all do good."
(PT Barnum)

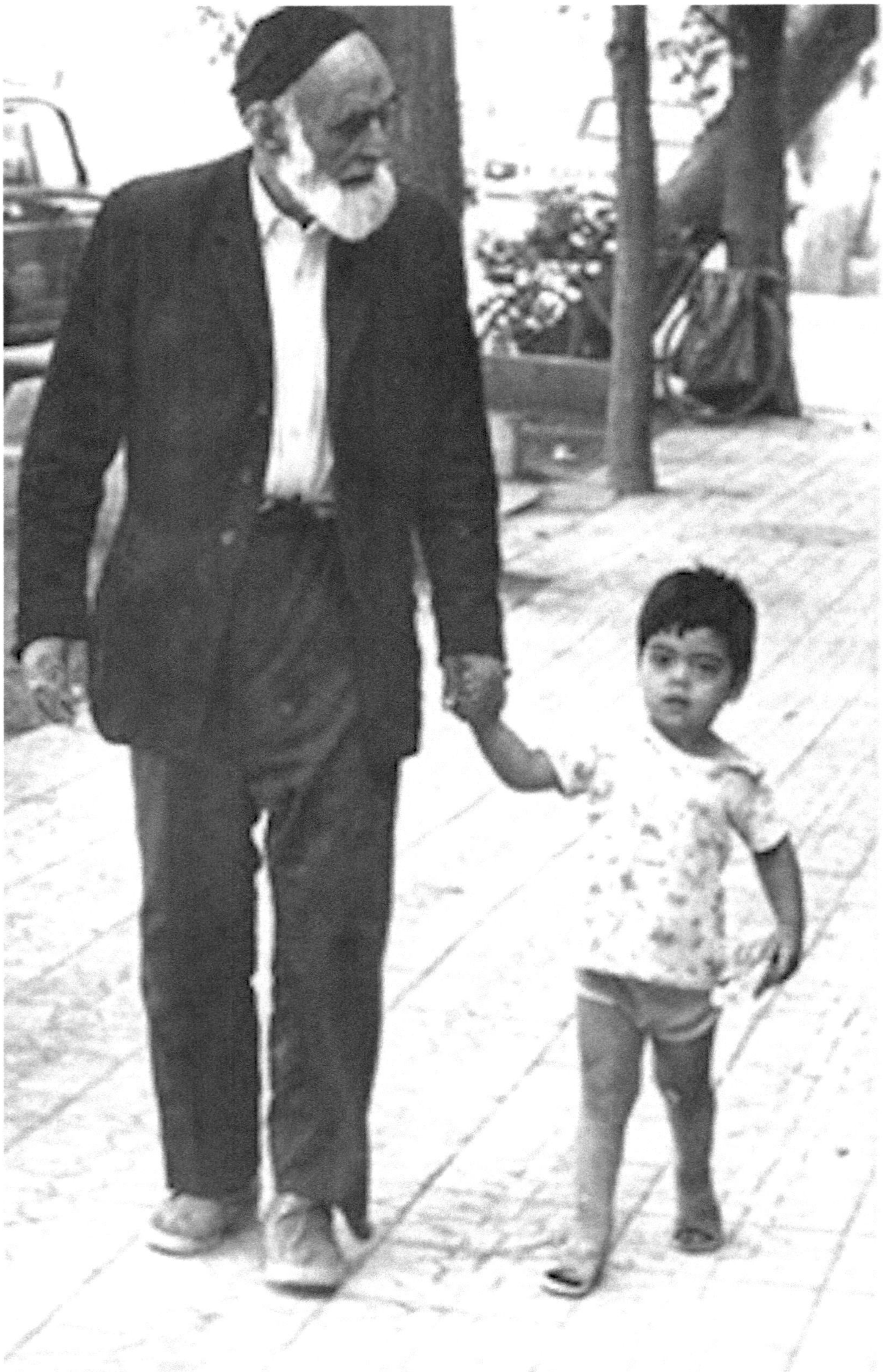

At some time or another we may be down on our luck
Or due to life circumstances, we are feeling a bit stuck

It helps to reach out to a trusted mentor
Someone to advise us who has been there before

Life can be like the roll of a dice
We are empowered when we ask for advice

Ingest every morsel of wisdom we receive
Guidance is all around if we simply perceive

"Literature is one of the most interesting and significant expressions of humanity." (PT Barnum)

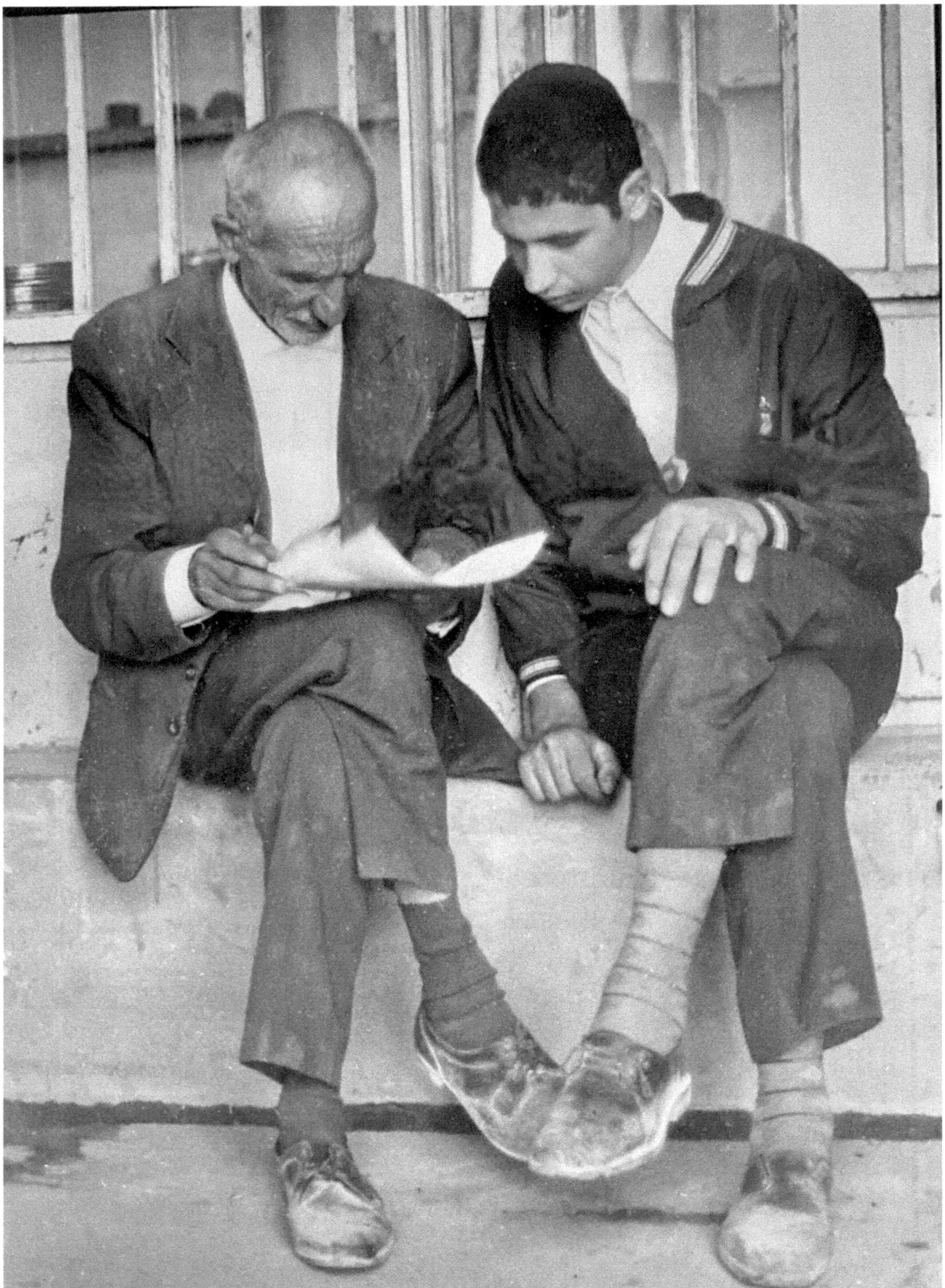

Take advice from those who've achieved their objectives
There is so much to learn from their perspectives

The failures they've encountered along the way
Are valuable learning lessons to convey

Their accomplishments are to be admired
And their learned wisdom is truly inspired

Assimilate the generous insight they share with you
So you know going forward what not to do

"Whatever you do, do it with all your might." (PT Barnum)

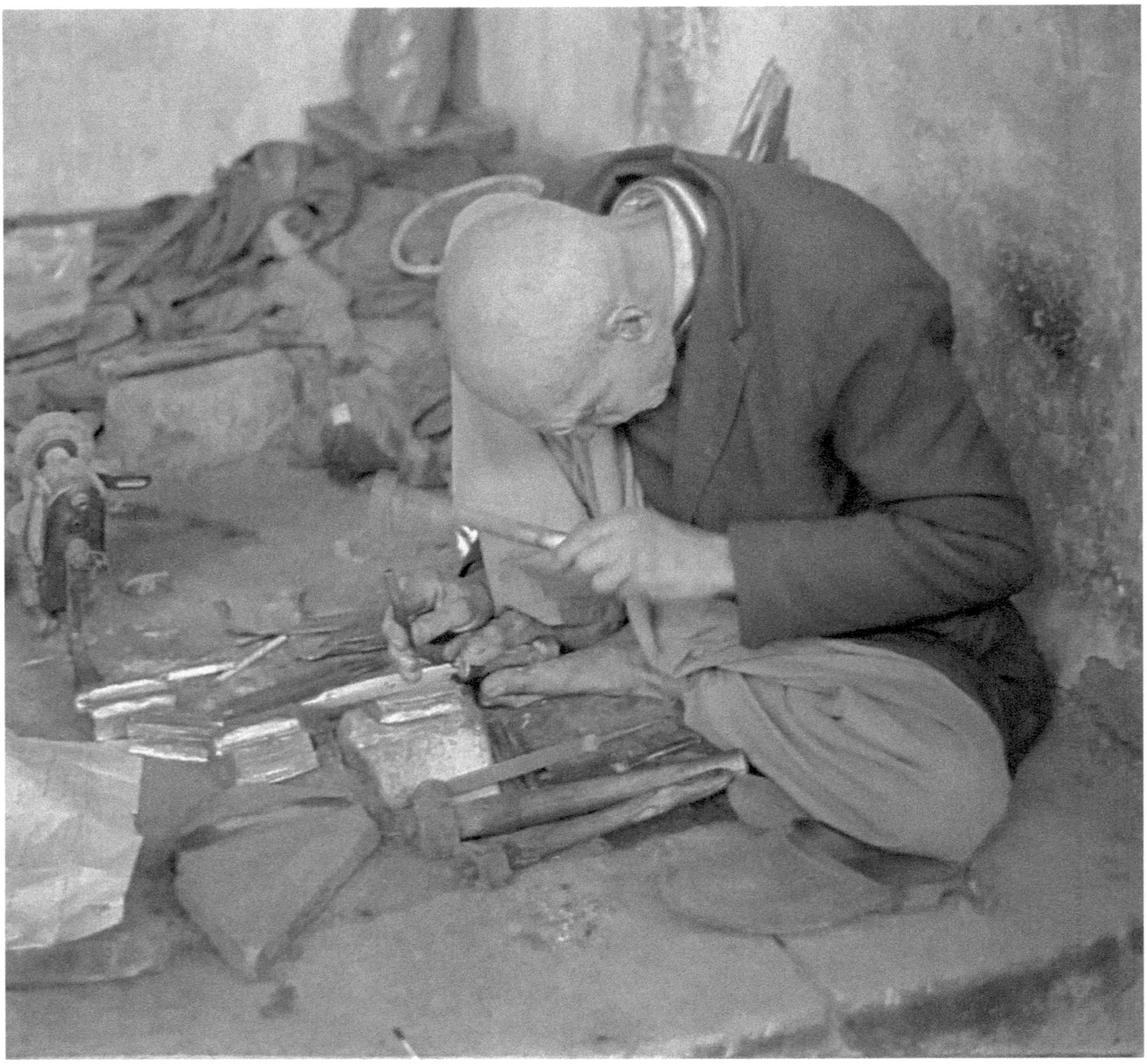

There is something to learn from everyone we meet
Missed opportunities can make us incomplete

From those who work with their hands, we learn how to create
From those who've achieved their dreams, we learn to emulate

What about those people who are annoying or demanding?
Perhaps the lessons learned are patience and understanding

When we come across people with different points of view
We should listen with an open mind so we don't misconstrue

"Go in confidence, study the rules,
and above all things, study human nature." (PT Barnum)

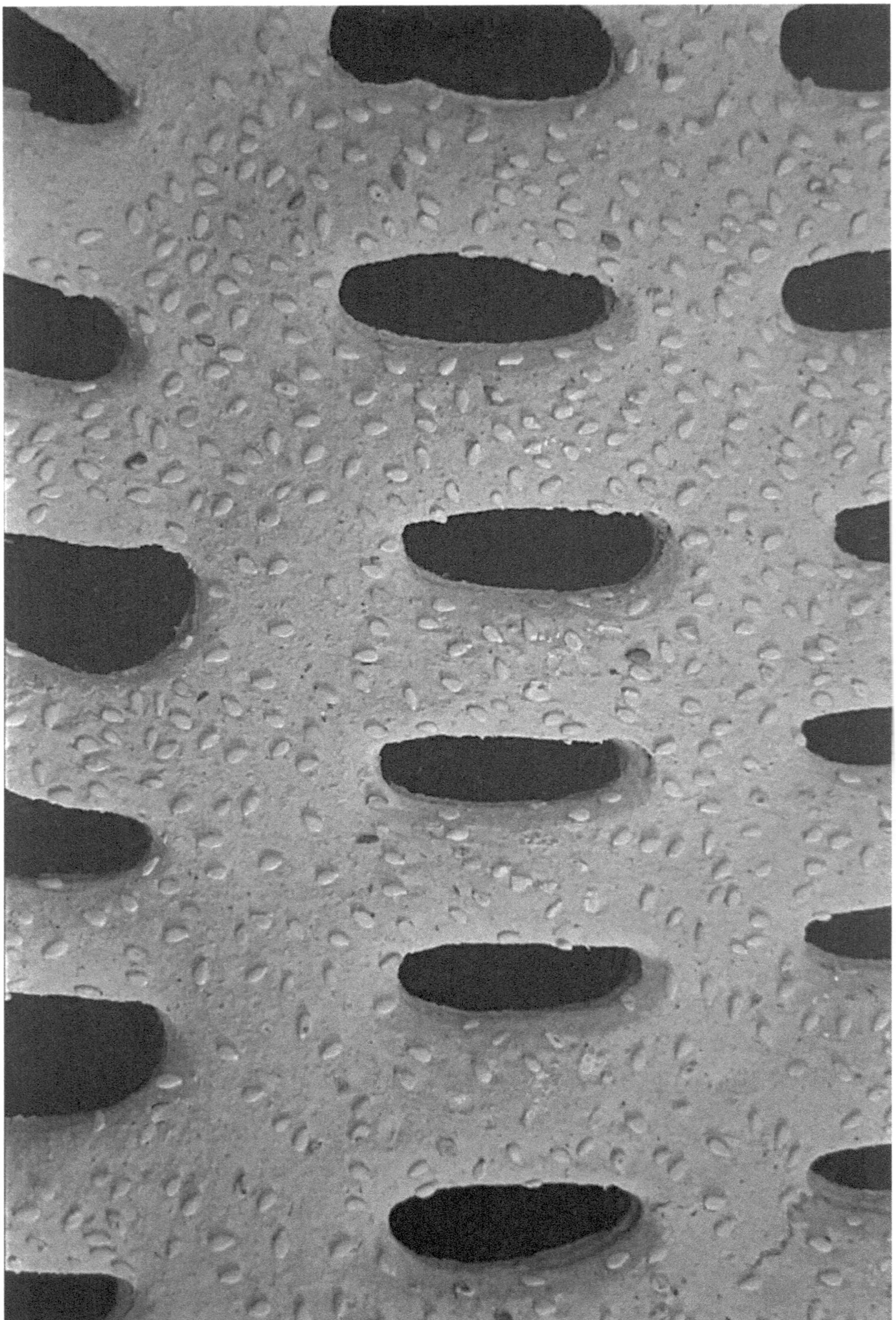

"Give us this day our daily bread"
That is the prayer that Jesus said

Those who count calories or are gluten free
May be concerned, but they needn't be

It is not literally bread that Jesus inferred
It's daily prayer and following His word

God gave us an instruction book to navigate through life
Imagine living in peace instead of in strife

"If he worthily fulfills his mission and amuses without corrupting, he need never feel that he has lived in vain." (PT Barnum)

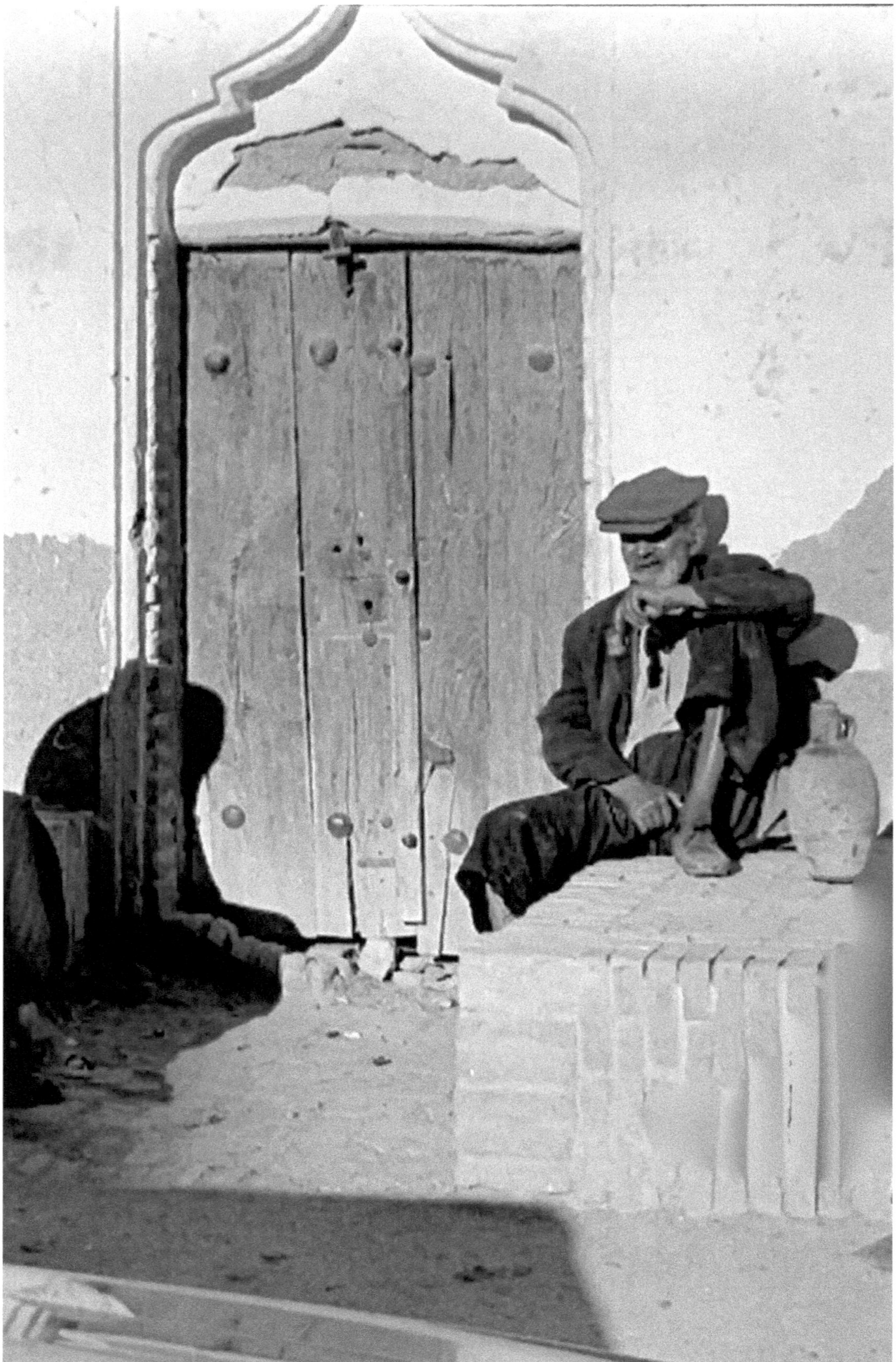

We've heard Lao Tzu's quote about teaching a man to fish
Success doesn't come about just by making a wish

It takes practice to become skilled at whatever we do
Persistence is key, then prosperity will ensue

Endurance encourages character, as well as intellect
Which in turn will provide us with much earned respect

Entitlements don't favor us in the long run
Real satisfaction comes from a job well done

" 'I will loose my camel and trust it to God!'
'No, no, not so,' said the prophet,
'Tie thy camel and trust it to God!' " (PT Barnum)

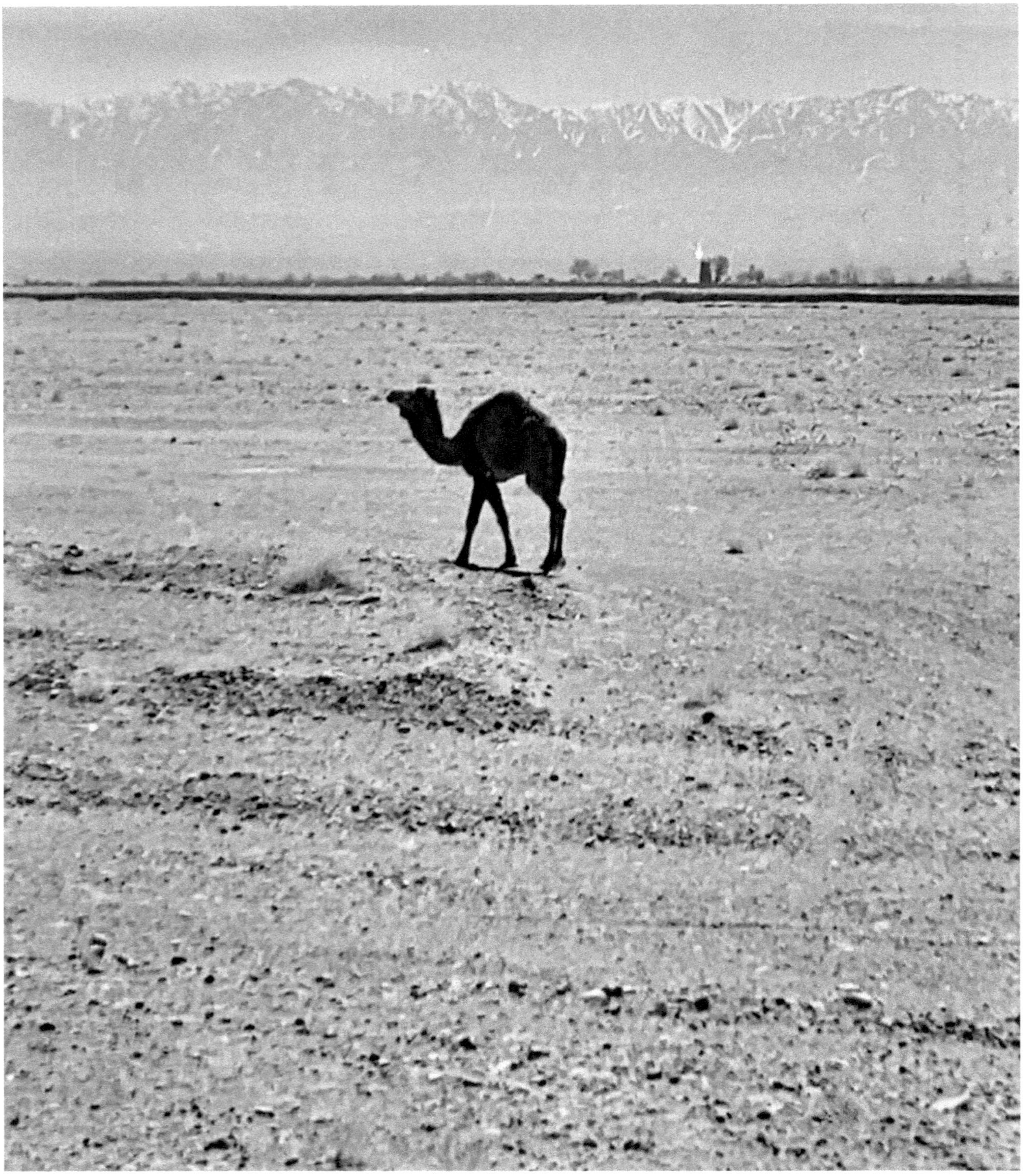

Saving our money for a rainy day is good advice financially
But if we also save our burdens, it will affect us substantially

Carrying around anger, resentment, and anxiety
Doesn't serve us well personally or within society

Make better use of our time and release all negativity
And focus our attention on active productivity

Concentrate on self-improvement instead of on what we lack
So we don't go through life with baggage on our back

"You will find there is more satisfaction in rational saving than in irrational spending." (PT Barnum)

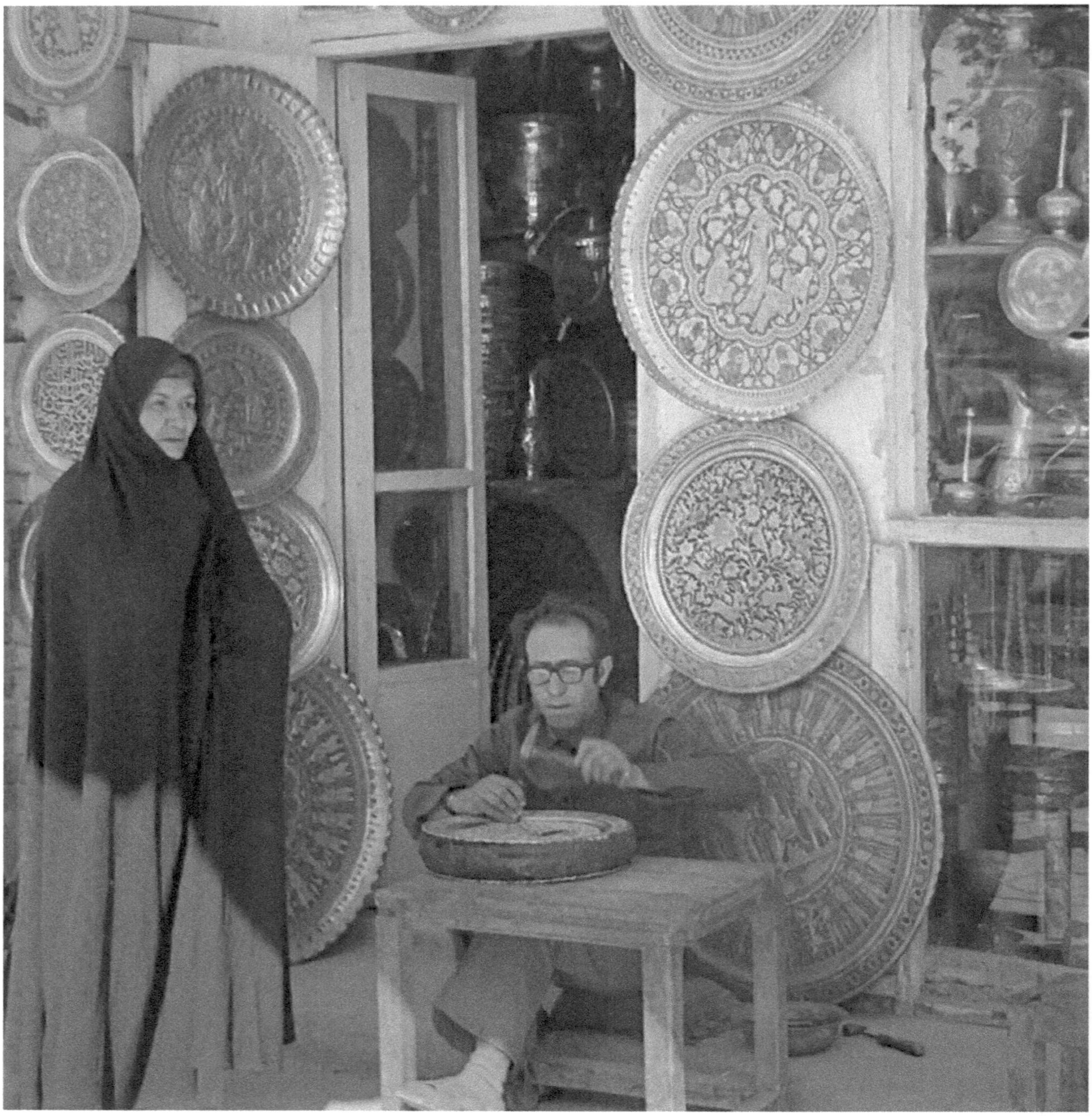

"You can't take it with you"... we've heard that said before
With regard to material possessions, why do we need more?

Let's collect memories in life, not things that cause clutter
And perhaps those experiences will cause our hearts to flutter

Spend quality time with family and friends
Treasure those moments... we don't know when they'll end

Leave smiles behind, from kind things that we've done
And appreciate life with all our loved ones

"Clowns are the pegs on which the circus is hung."
(PT Barnum)

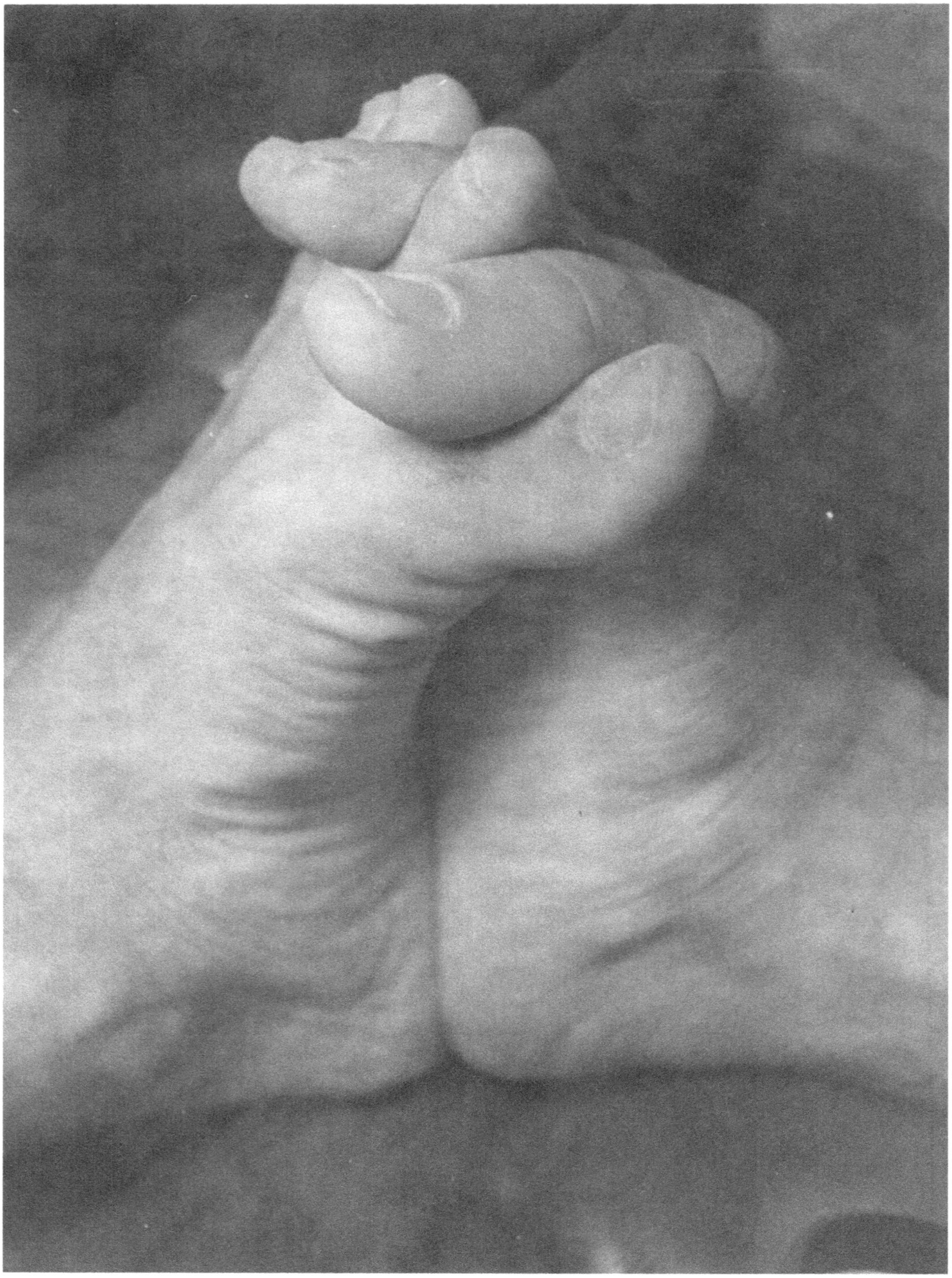

This photo may seem bizarre compared to all the rest
But my brother was quite witty, of that I can attest

"Why feet?" you may ask, a valid question indeed
And no, my brother was not smoking weed

He liked to have fun and make people laugh
So here is a silly page on his behalf

Without something comical, this book would be incomplete
So when life gives you bunions, I hope you'll think of my brother's feet

"When was the last time you smiled?
Or had a good laugh?" (PT Barnum)

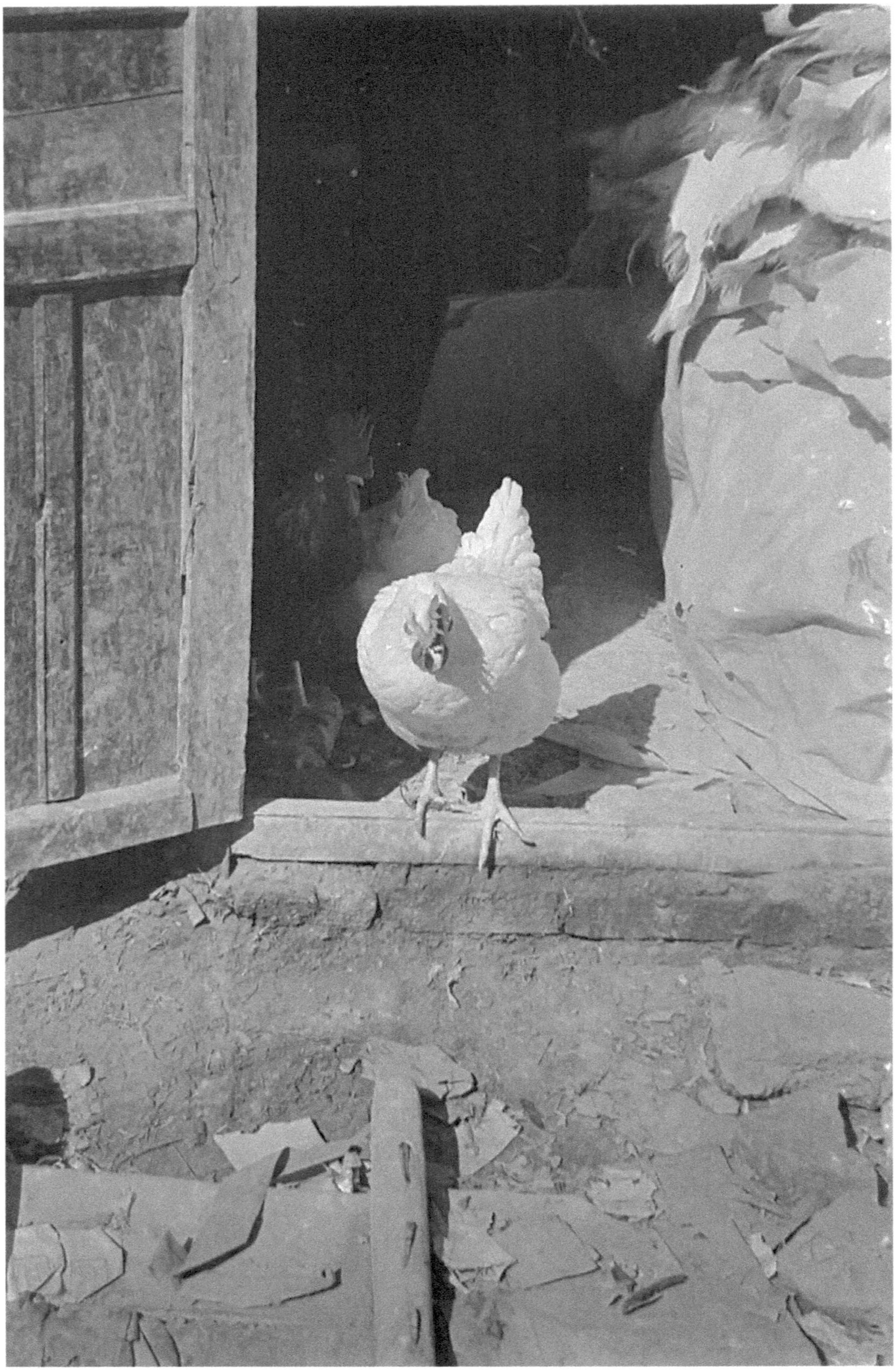

Laughter is healing and makes life worthwhile
As simple as it sounds, it all starts with a smile

Did you hear about the chicken who had to move to another abode?
She kept getting asked why she was crossing the road

Why did everyone expect her to explain
The constant questions nearly drove her insane

She broke up with the rooster with whom she was having a tryst
And now she is seeing a therapist

"Let your motto then always be 'Excelsior,'
for by living up to it there is no such word as fail." (PT Barnum)

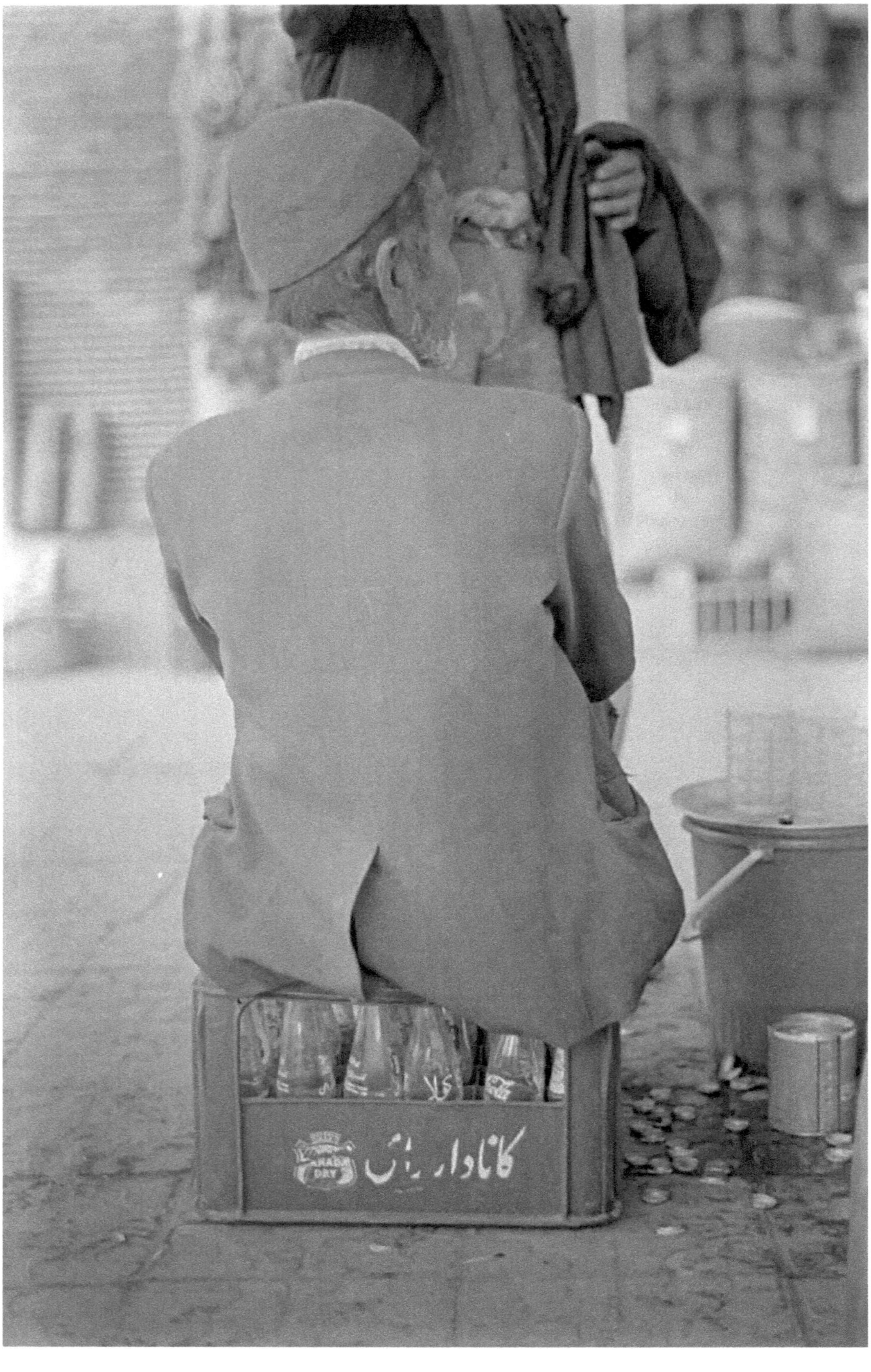

The bottle we saw earlier is now overflowing
And as it replenishes, it continues growing

Our thoughts totally affect the life we create
We have complete control when our minds are in state

Once we learn to live with intention
There is no limit to our circumvention

Life really can be all we imagine
If we just learn to follow our passion

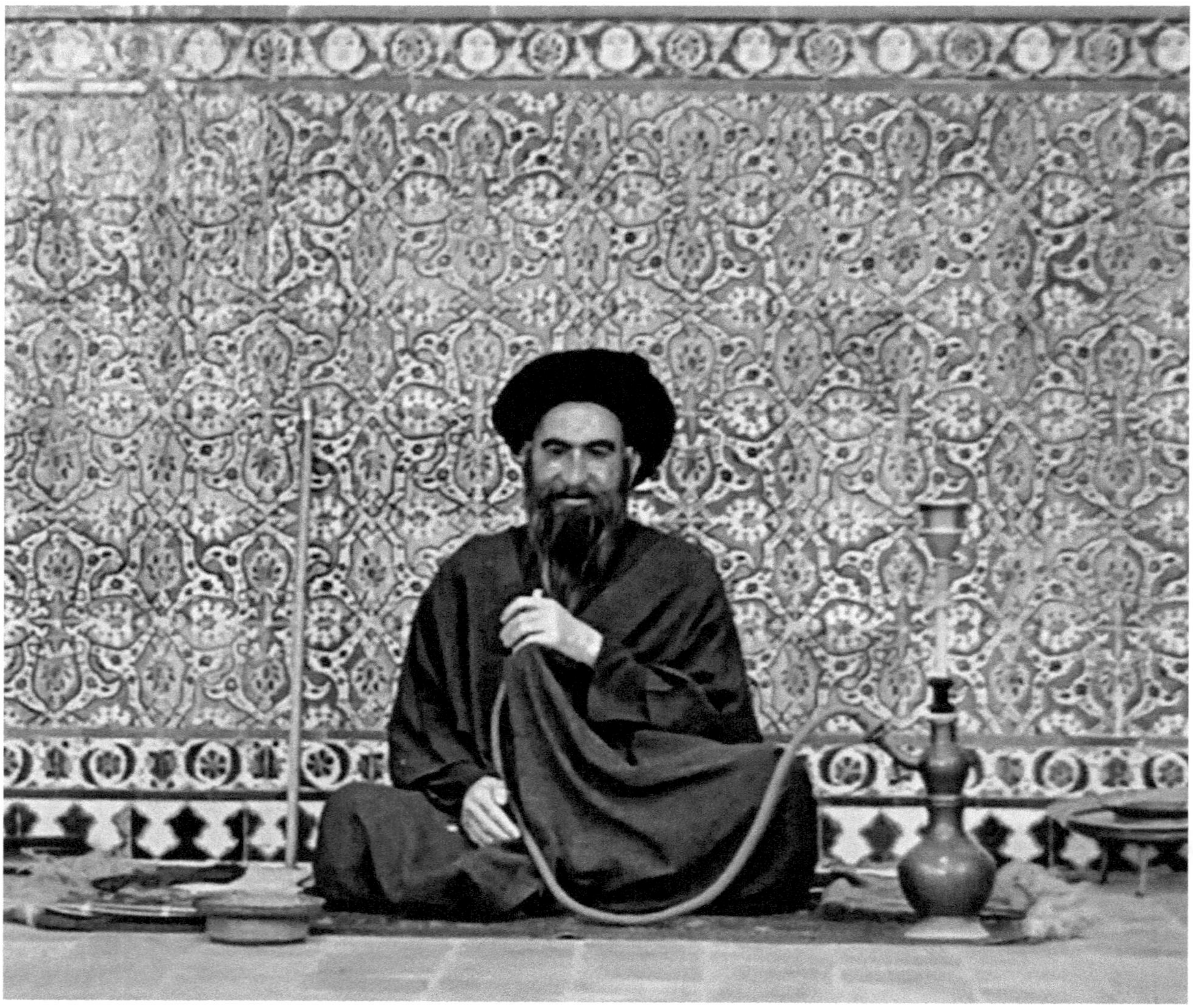

Conclusion

When I found out about my brother's terminal illness, I was an emotional mess. I couldn't understand why it happened, and to be honest, I still don't. However, I've learned that God has a reason for every experience we have in life, and every trial is meant to strengthen our faith. While we can't always control what happens in life, we *can* control how we react to it. Our external circumstances cannot control us unless we allow them. I am grateful for every experience, good and bad. When life is good, I appreciate it…When it's not, I choose to learn from it…And it is definitely a choice.

I've read numerous inspirational books over the years, and many people refer to their message as the Law of Attraction. What some don't realize is that the Law of Attraction actually originated from the Bible:

- "For as he thinks in his heart, so is he." Proverbs 23:7
- "According to your faith, shall it be done to you." Matthew 9:29
- "And all things, whatsoever you shall ask in prayer, believing, you shall receive." Matthew 21:22

This book is no exception, and I hope that I have been able to embody that message.

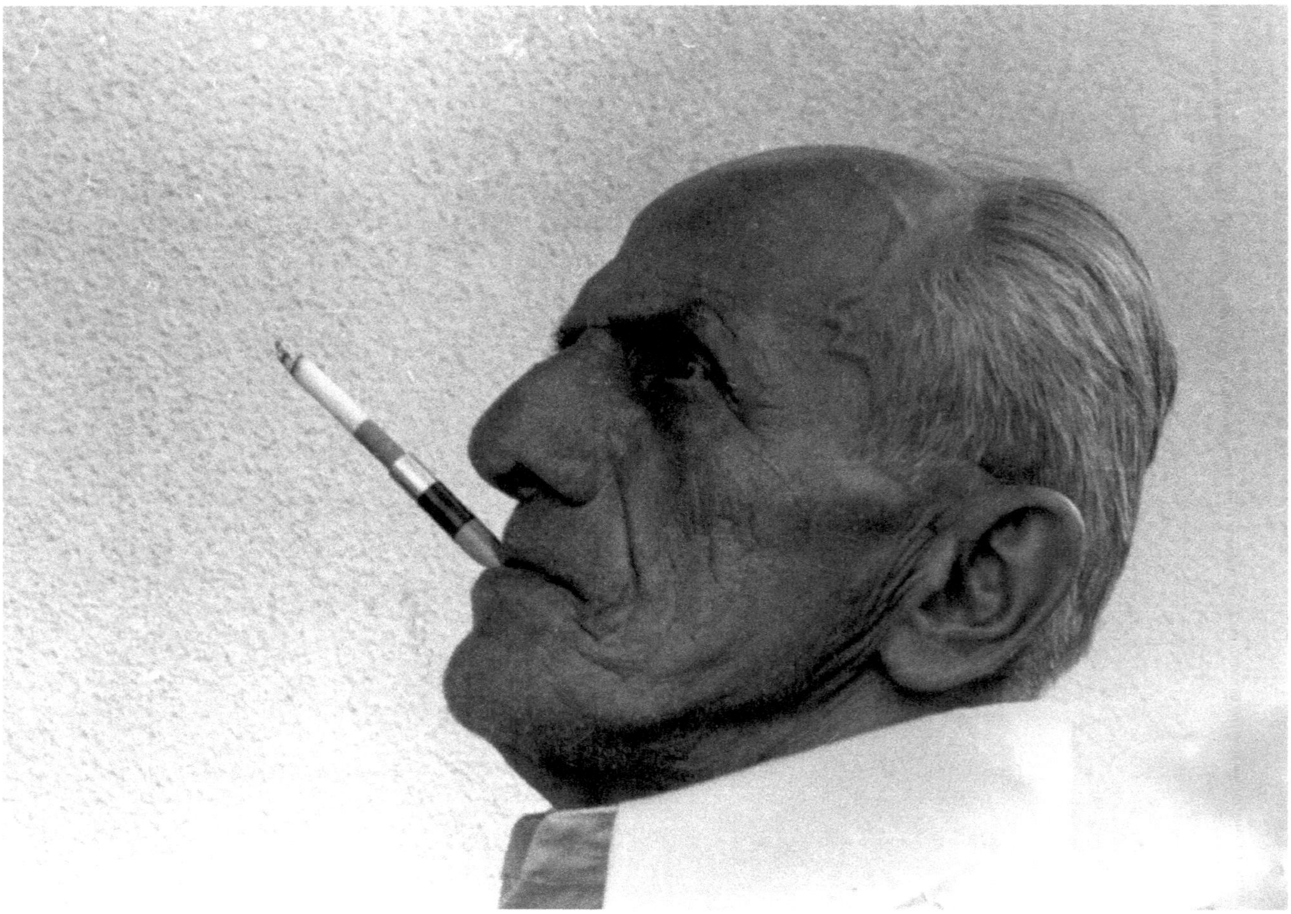

Printed in the USA
CPSIA information can be obtained
at www.ICGtesting.com
CBHW042101310724
12432CB00035B/910

9 798890 419132